Handbook for the Accused
Second Edition

J. Anthony Bryan & Roger Lampkin

Roger Lampkin – (661)633-1234
1234 L Street
Bakersfield, CA 93301

J. Anthony Bryan – (661)861-8050
1412 17th St., Ste. 340
Bakersfield, CA 93301

Copyright © 2017 Legal Research Services
P.O. Box 81
Bakersfield, CA 93302
(661)Justice (587-8423)
All rights reserved.

A portion of the royalties from this book
will be donated to charities assisting the accused.

ISBN: 1975817168
ISBN-13: 978-1975817169

TABLE OF CONTENTS

A. Acknowledgements vi
B. Introduction 1
C. Important Terms 7
D. Answers to bail Questions 18
    1. What is bail? 18
    2. Do I have to post bail if I can prove I am innocent? 18
    3. Can the amount of bail be reduced? 18
    4. What does the court consider when setting bail? 18
    5. What is cash bail? 19
    6. What is a real estate bond? 19
    7. What is a bail bond? 20
    8. How much does a bail bond cost? 20
    9. What is a bail source hearing? 20
    10. When do I get bail back? 21
    11. Do I get back the money I paid for a bail bond? 21
    12. What do I get back from the bondsman? 21
    13. What is a cosigner responsible for? 21
E. Order of hearings 22
    1. Felony 22
    2. Misdemeanor 22
F. Help your attorney 23
    1. Introduction 23
    2. Don't sabotage your defense 26
    3. Cooperate with your defense team 27
G. Replace your attorney 29
    1. Introduction 29
    2. Hire a different attorney 29
    3. Ask your attorney to declare a conflict 29
    4. Ask the court to give you a new attorney 29
    5. Represent Yourself 30

- H. Immigration Consequences 31
  1. General Deportation Rules 31
  2. Aggravated Felony 34
  3. Crime of Violence 37
  4. Crime Involving Moral Turpitude 38
  5. Controlled Substance Offense 38
- I. Motions before trial 40
  1. Introduction 40
  2. Notice requirements 41
- J. Sample motions before trial 43
  Introduction 43
  1. Continuance 44
  2. Compel Discovery 47
  3. Bail 57
  4. Lineup 61
  5. Suppress 67
  6. Set Aside the Information 70
  7. Recall Warrant 76
  8. Pitchess 78
  9. Withdraw Plea 82
  10. Prohibit Restrictions on Right to Counsel 84
  11. Traverse 87
  12. Disclose Informant 92
  13. Unseal Affidavit (Hitch Motion) 98
  14. Enforce Agreement 103
  15. Sanctions (Trombetta Motion) 106
  16. Dismiss for Speedy Trial Violation 110
  17. Dismiss for Delay in Prosecution 113
  18. Set Motions Date 118
  19. Joinder 120
  20. Substitute Counsel (Marsden) 121
- K. Ex parte pleadings 123
- L. Sample ex parte pleadings 124

	1. Order Shortening Time 124
	2. Removal Order 126
	3. Motion to Appoint Expert 128
	4. Motion to Appoint Paralegal 133
M.	Trial (in limine) motions 139
N.	Sample trial (in limine) motions 141
	1. Omnibus Motion in Limine 141
	2. Motion in Limine to Exclude Prejudicial Evidence 145
	3. Motion in Limine to Federalize Objections 147
O.	Objections 152
P.	Sample Letters 155
	1. Offer to assist 155
	2. Request for suppression 155
	3. Request for discovery 156
	4. Request for testing 156
	5. Request to disclose conflicts 157
	6. Request to declare conflict 157
	7. Request for dismissal 158
Q.	Select legal authorities 159
	Evidence Code §350 159
	Evidence Code §351 159
	Evidence Code §352 159
	Evidence Code §402 159
	Evidence Code §1200 159
	Penal Code §995 160
	Penal Code §1054.1 160
	Penal Code §1382 161
	Penal Code §1473 162
	Penal Code §1538.5 163
R.	About the authors 164

A. ACKNOWLEDGEMENTS

Many of the pleadings in this book are simplified versions of pleadings filed in the various California Courts. Others were created based on specific statutes or case law, and still others were taken from ideas discussed by members of the legal community. Some of the pleadings, such as the Motion in Limine to Federalize Objections, have been filed in many different forms by many different attorneys in many different cases. As such, the original source of much of this material is unknown and full credit to the original authors cannot be given. Nonetheless, we will attempt to do so here.

Pleadings and ideas for pleadings have been gleaned from many fine attorneys, including Bill Slocumb, Andrew Fishkin, David Faulkner, Larry Fields, Elliot Magnus, Joe Whittington, and Richard Jackson.

Special thanks to proofreader Haily Steinhilber.

Would you like to be included here? Send your favorite motions, quotes, practice pointers, and ideas to Admin@HelpGettingOff.com.

B. INTRODUCTION

If you are accused of a crime in California, it will harm you for the rest of your life. Once accused, you can never win. The charges may be reduced. The charges may be dismissed. You may be given a dismissal in exchange for better treatment, or you may receive some other minimal sentence. You may even be found not guilty, but before your case ends you will suffer fear, stress, and possibly an extended incarceration.

If you have money, you will probably be required to spend it. Your friends and family may shun you, and you will constantly have to answer the question, "what did you do?" If you are innocent, few people will believe you. Even your attorney may presume you are guilty.

If you don't fight for your rights, your attorney may pressure you into a quick plea bargain so he is free to move on to the next case. Worse yet, you might not even be given an attorney. If you don't hire an attorney or ask for one, the court might pressure you into a quick plea bargain. There are countless sad examples of what can happen to a defendant who does not take the time to understand the legal system and assert his rights.

Michael is a sad example.

Michael, a professional photographer, was rapidly snapping pictures of an underage girl when she flung open her top, exposing her breasts. Michael deleted the last few frames he had shot, instructed the girl to clothe herself, and went on with the photo shoot. Later in the day, the girl demanded that Michael give her the pictures so she could share them with her boyfriend. Michael could not comply since the pictures had been deleted, so the girl called law enforcement and reported the theft of her pictures.

A police raid and extremely thorough search ensued, but no nude pictures were found on Michael's cameras, on Michael's computers, or anywhere at all. There were no nude pictures - no nude pictures of the girl who was accusing him, no nude pictures of anyone at all. Nevertheless, Michael was arrested and charged with Annoying or Molesting a Child, *Penal Code §647.6*, a misdemeanor sex offense.

Michael hired an expensive out-of-town attorney, but the attorney didn't show up for court. An associate came to court and asked for more time to prepare for trial. At the next hearing, a different attorney showed up and again asked for more time.

No one was actually preparing for trial. The attorneys were simply "seasoning" the case, a common practice in which attorneys stall and delay until the defendant finally gives up and accepts a plea bargain.

After a bit more seasoning, Michael's attorney finally came to court. Even though Michael had not committed a crime, the attorney convinced Michael that a trial would be risky and expensive. The high-dollar-huckster went on to minimize the consequences of a conviction, and told Michael that the attorney had negotiated a fantastic deal.

Under the *guiding hand of learned counsel*, Michael pled guilty as charged.

It was later that Michael learned his conviction would require him to register as a sex offender for the rest of his life.

Brianna is a sad example.

Brianna's father began giving her alcohol at a very young age so she wouldn't resist as much when he raped her. She didn't finish high school because she was usually too drunk to learn, and her father often kept her home to use for his own pleasure. After many years, Brianna's father was arrested and sent away forever, and Brianna was a chronic alcoholic.

It was inevitable that Brianna would eventually be picked up for Driving Under the Influence (DUI); she was always under the influence of alcohol. Her first two DUI cases seemed to go favorably. At her arraignments, her "attorney" told her that he had a great deal: no jail time if she pleads guilty. Brianna didn't realize that the person she believed to be her attorney was actually a probation officer. Some jurisdictions have probation officers come to arraignment to assist defendants, but the assistance is often simply convincing defendants to take a quick plea and lessen court congestion. Brianna took the deal each time. She lost her driving privileges and had to spend a few days picking up trash in the county's work release program.

Brianna was an alcoholic, and the criminal justice system made little effort to help her recover. There was no inquiry into the reason for her alcoholism. Even before finishing her work release time, Brianna again had a bottle in her hand.

For her third DUI, Brianna lucked out and got a real attorney – a real good attorney. Her public defender was fairly new and inexperienced, but he made up for it in effort. He studied her case. He studied the law. He realized that there were problems with Brianna's first two cases. A probation officer can't masquerade as an attorney to lure defendants into pleading guilty. It is enough of an error to have both convictions overturned.

He also realized that having the convictions overturned might do little more than set Brianna up for three back-to-back DUI trials. If he had the cases overturned, there was a danger that the District Attorney would take all three cases to trial. He used this knowledge to strike a sweet deal for Brianna. By statute, Brianna faced a minimum of 120 days in jail, but the prosecutor asked for 180 days. This skilled public defender convinced the prosecutor to agree that Brianna's first DUI was invalid. Brianna entered a plea to a second time DUI and was sentenced to "time served." Her only time in jail was the time she waited to enter her plea.

Brianna's luck ran out with her fourth DUI. She was assigned a "public pretender." It would be generous to say Brianna's attorney glanced at the file, but she probably didn't even do that. Instead, the attorney told Brianna that, as a hopeless drunk with a high blood alcohol level, there was no hope.

Brianna told the attorney about the earlier agreement that her first plea was invalid, but the attorney didn't want to be bothered with an actual defense. Each successive DUI carries harsher punishment, and the attorney told Brianna to plead guilty to a fourth time DUI, even though Brianna legally could have, at most, been convicted of a third time DUI. A fourth time DUI is a felony, so the conviction will haunt Brianna for the rest of her life. Brianna went to prison, and she will never again enjoy all of her civil rights.

There is no good excuse for Brianna's conduct. She was drunk and she drove – at least four times. There is also no excuse for what the criminal justice system did to Brianna. Even an alcoholic is entitled to a defense. Every defendant is entitled to a defense.

Jason is a sad example.

One rainy day, a small car was speeding down the highway when a large truck pulled up along the passenger side. The driver of the truck stuck a gun out the window, and fired one shot. The bullet went through the car passenger's eye and into his brain. Death was instant.

A tip, most probably from the real killer, led the police to Jason. An eyewitness, the driver of the car, was given a photo lineup with Jason in the cherished number two slot. Other people in the lineup were in regular clothes. Jason was in prison garb and was standing in front of a column of height numbers. The driver still didn't identify Jason as the shooter.

The police showed the driver a photograph of Jason, and then did a live lineup. The driver still didn't choose Jason.

At trial, the driver positively identified Jason as the shooter. There was almost no additional evidence to implicate Jason. The case was based almost entirely on the driver's in court identification, but Jason's attorney made no mention of the driver's inability to identify Jason during earlier attempts. The attorney also didn't mention that it was raining on the day of the shooting, and the attorney didn't even realize that because of the height difference between the car and the truck, it would have been nearly impossible for the driver of the car to have seen the perpetrator's face.

The passenger in the shooter's truck had previously testified and identified the actual shooter, which was not Jason, but Jason's attorney didn't bother to call the passenger to testify at trial. Jason's attorney didn't put on any affirmative defense whatsoever because he was so sure that he had won Jason's case. The attorney lost the case, but it was really Jason who lost.

Jason was convicted and sentenced to life in prison.

Raise your hand!

In each of these sad examples, the defendant could have done something to protect his or her rights, but each passively sat by as the attorneys failed them.

Michael knew that he was innocent. Michael knew that his attorney wasn't prepared. Had Michael raised his hand and asked for a new attorney, his name probably wouldn't be in this book.

Brianna knew that one of her prior convictions had already been deemed invalid. Brianna's attorney knew it too, but instead of informing the court, the attorney demeaned Brianna and told her to plead guilty so she could get help. Brianna didn't get help; she got convicted. Had Brianna raised her hand and told the judge that at least one of her convictions was invalid, perhaps the judge would have at least asked the attorney about it. It is unlikely that the attorney would have said, "yes, her earlier conviction was invalid, but she's a drunk, so let's not worry about it."

Jason knew about the failed eyewitness identification, and Jason knew about the eyewitness who had cleared him. Jason knew that his attorney wasn't going to put on any defense, but Jason sat idly by and watched it happen. If Jason had raised his hand and told the judge what was happening, perhaps the judge would have stepped in and informed the jury that the eye witness had never before identified Jason as the shooter. Perhaps the judge would have asked Jason's attorney why he had not called the other eyewitness to clear Jason.

If you went to the doctor with the sniffles and the doctor told you he wanted to amputate your arm, you wouldn't stretch out your arm and ask him to be quick about it. If you went to the mechanic for a simple oil change and he told you he needed to change your entire engine, you wouldn't reach for your wallet just yet. If your barber wanted to try to cut your hair with his new lawnmower, you would probably be a bit hesitant to start, yet no matter how poorly an attorney performs, many defendants keep silent and go along with whatever the attorney advises.

Purpose

This book is written for the defendant wishing to help in his own defense. It discusses the general progression of cases, common terms that are used, and it contains examples of common pretrial motions that that are often used to further the defense.

Much of the information in here can easily be found on the Internet, but the book is written under the presumption that most readers will be in custody and not have Internet access. The book, therefore, also has blank sections for notes. However, a defendant who is in custody should use caution in taking notes because the book may fall into the hands of guards or other inmates. Don't write anything that can be used against you.

Many sample documents are included. The samples as a general guide as to some common types of motions your attorney might bring. Motions are largely case specific, and there are many different ways to state the same motion. The motions in this book are not a rigid formula that will always succeed. In court, there is nothing that always succeeds, and the prejudice against defendants is so extreme that any attempt at justice will be an uphill battle.

This book is intended to provide accurate and authoritative information about the subject matter covered, but it is in no way a comprehensive guide. Use of this book does not create an attorney-client relationship with any of the authors or contributors, and this book is distributed with the understanding that the authors, publishers, and distributors do not render legal advice through this book. If legal advice or other expert assistance is required, seek the services of a professional.

Persons using this book in dealing with specific legal matters should exercise their own independent judgment and conduct their own independent research. Because the law changes on a daily basis, this book, like almost every other law book, is out of date. Every effort has been made to ensure the accuracy of this book on the day of printing, but there is simply no way the printed word can morph to keep up with an ever-changing legal system, and no one can predict with certainty what any given court will do on any given day.

Additional Help

Consider obtaining copies of other books by these same authors, such as *California Criminal Defense Motions in Limine*, *Sex Registration Guidebook*, or *Criminal Defense Guide to Facebook*.

Both authors are available for consultation on a variety of topics. Roger Lampkin may be reached at 661-633-1234, and J. Anthony Bryan may be reached at 661-861-8050 or by e-mail at Attorney@JAnthonyBryan.com.

Major contributors to this book are also available for consultation.
- Bill Slocumb – (661)324-1400
- Joe Whittington – (661)322-5833
- Andrew Fishkin – (661)322-6776
- David Faulkner – (661)324-4777
- Larry Fields – (661)861-9750
- Elliot Magnus – (661)395-0240

C. IMPORTANT TERMS

The explanations given here are greatly simplified. Some of the terms have wide use in a legal setting, but the explanations provided are limited to the application in criminal proceedings.

Accessory

Someone who helps another person commit a crime or hide the fact that a crime has been committed. An accessory is usually not physically present during the crime.

Accomplice

Someone who helps a person commit a crime. An accomplice is guilty the same as if he personally committed the offense. Example: a getaway driver.

Appeal

An appeal is a review of a case by a higher court. Felony convictions in Superior Court are reviewed by the Court of Appeal. Misdemeanor convictions in Superior Court may be reviewed by the Appellate Division of the Superior Court or by the Court of Appeal. An appeal can only be taken from a from a final order of the court. Interim orders, such as rulings on motions, are generally not appealable (see Writ). Final orders include rulings such as:
1. Verdict after court or jury trial *(Penal Code §1237(a))*
2. Ruling on a contested violation of probation *(Penal Code §1237(b))*
3. Denial of a motion to suppress evidence, but only after the defendant is otherwise convicted *(Penal Code §1538.5(m))*
4. An improper sentence after a valid plea *(Rules of Court, rule 8.304(b))*
5. An improper calculation of custody credits, but only if "the defendant first presents the claim in the trial court at the time of sentencing, or if the error is not discovered until after sentencing [and] the defendant first makes a motion for correction of the record in the trial court" *(Penal Code §1237.1)*
6. A plea bargain, but only if "The defendant has filed with the trial court a written statement, executed under oath or penalty of perjury showing reasonable constitutional, jurisdictional, or other grounds going to the legality of the proceedings. [and] The trial court has executed and filed a certificate of probable cause for such appeal with the clerk of the court." *(Penal Code §1237.5)*

Acquittal

A finding that the defendant is not guilty.

Arraignment

An arraignment is the proceeding where a defendant is advised of the charges against him and he enters a plea to the charges. If the defendant is already represented by an attorney, reading of the charges will usually be waived.

The most common pleas are "guilty," "not guilty," and "no contest." A defendant may also demurrer to the charges or enter a plea of not guilty by reason of insanity. A "no contest" plea is treated the same as a "guilty" plea for most purposes.

The arraignment often involves other matters, such as:
- The court may ask the defendant if he can afford an attorney, and the court will appoint an attorney for the defendant.
- The Public Defender or other assigned attorney may declare a conflict and request that a different attorney be assigned to the defendant.
- The court may play a video recording explaining defendants' rights and the court process.
- The court may set or change bail.
- The court may set future court dates.
- Defendant or his attorney may request discovery from the court or from the District Attorney, and discovery may be provided.

Arbuckle Waiver

If a defendant enters a plea, the judge who takes the plea must be the sentencing judge unless the defendant waives that right. The waiver of the right to have the plea judge be the sentencing judge is called an Arbuckle Waiver.

Bench Trial

A trial by the judge alone without a jury.

Boykin/Tahl Advisement

Before a defendant enters a plea of guilty or no contest, the court is required to ensure that the plea is knowing and voluntary. The court must (1) advise defendant of his constitutional rights to a jury trial, to confront witnesses against him, and against self-incrimination, and (2) obtain defendant's waivers of those rights.

These rules were established in the cases of *Boykin v. Alabama* (1969) 395 U.S. 238, 243-244 (*Boykin*) and *In re Tahl* (1969) 1 Cal. 3rd 122, 130-133 (*Tahl*).

A failure to give these admonishments and obtain waivers may still be harmless if the record shows the plea was voluntary and intelligent under the totality of the circumstances, but most courts orally give the Boykin/Tahl Advisement along with other advisements or the court may require the defendant to complete and sign a form containing the advisements.

Circumstantial Evidence

Evidence that requires an inference. This is generally all evidence other than eyewitness testimony regarding the actual crime. Examples: fingerprints, DNA, a witness who sees the defendant near the crime scene.

Complaint

A Complaint is the initial charging document. It contains a list of the charges and enhancements against the defendant. (See "Information")

Concurrent Sentence

Sentences for different crimes are served at the same time. Example, a two year sentence concurrent with a four year sentence would only require the defendant to serve the four year sentence.

Consecutive Sentence

Sentences for different crimes are served one after another. Example, a two year sentence consecutive to a four year sentence would require the defendant to serve the four year sentence then serve the two year sentence.

Continuance

A continuance is a request for more time. It is a request that the court move a hearing to a later date.

Conference

Conferences are generally for two purposes – negotiate a settlement and/or set dates for additional hearings. Conferences go by many names, such as Preliminary Hearing Setting Conference, Pre-Preliminary Hearing, Status Conference, Readiness Conference, or Trial Setting Conference.

Cruz Waiver

A Cruz Waiver allows a defendant to be released from jail pending sentencing based on his promise to appear for sentencing. The waiver is made after a defendant enters into a plea bargain. If the defendant fails to appear for sentencing, he may receive a sentence greater than the one agreed to in the plea bargain. The maximum allowable sentence for the charges pled to may be imposed even if that sentence is greater than that allowed by the original plea bargain.

Deferred Entry of Judgment

The defendant enters a plea, but is not sentenced until a future date. If the defendant meets certain requirements by that date (complete a drug program, complete anger management classes, etc.) the case will be dismissed or the sentence reduced depending on the terms of the original plea bargain.

Demurrer

A demurrer (demur for short) is document claiming that the allegations in the document charging defendant (the Complaint or Information) do not properly allege a crime. In other words, a demur claims that the defendant's conduct is not criminal and the case should be dismissed.

Discovery

The evidence concerning a case is called discovery.

Ducus Tecum

See "Subpoena"

Enhancement

A fact that if proven will increase the punishment for a crime. Common enhancements are personal use of a firearm, infliction of great bodily injury, or that the crime was committed for the benefit of a gang.

Ex Parte

A communication between one party and the court without involvement of the other party. As examples, police obtain an ex parte search warrant from the court – the defendant has no say in the matter. The defense obtains an ex parte order appointing a private investigator to assist with the case – the prosecution has no say in the matter.

Exculpatory

Evidence that helps the defendant is exculpatory. Evidence that tends to harm the defendant is inculpatory.

Grand Jury

A group of people appointed to hear evidence and determine if there is probable cause to believe that a crime has been committed and that the defendant has committed the crime. They meet secretly and have evidence presented to them by the District Attorney. Most cases in California are prosecuted using a Preliminary Hearing in front of a judge, but some cases still go before a Grand Jury.

Habeas Corpus

A Writ of Habeas Corpus, commonly referred to as simply Habeas Corpus, is an order to bring a person to court so that the court may determine whether it is proper to hold the person in custody. The document used to request the Writ is a Petition for Writ of Habeas Corpus, commonly called a Habeas Petition. There is rarely a reason to file a Habeas Petition before a defendant has been convicted and had his conviction reviewed on appeal.

Harvey Waiver

When sentencing a defendant, the judge is only allowed to consider the charges the defendant is actually convicted of. The judge cannot give any consideration to charges that have been dismissed. A Harvey Waiver abandons this rule and allows the judge to consider dismissed charges when deciding on an appropriate sentence.

Impeach

To discredit or show that a witness is incorrect. Impeachment may be done by showing the witness has reason to lie, such as asking, "the defendant is your brother, isn't he." Impeachment may also be done by showing the witness suffered from a physical disability that prevented him from observing or remembering events accurately, such as questioning the witness about his state of intoxication, his poor vision, or a mental disability that prevents him from remembering. Impeachment may also be done by showing that the witness suffers from felony convictions or other crimes of moral turpitude.

In Limine

A motion made in front of the trial judge shortly before the start of evidence in a trial.

Indictment

A document listing the charges against a defendant following a grand jury hearing.

Information

The charging document filed by the prosecution after a preliminary hearing. A defendant is initially charged using a Complaint. If the judge presiding over the preliminary hearing rules that there is sufficient evidence to believe that the defendant is guilty, the prosecution will be allowed to file an Information listing the charges against the defendant.

Limine
See "In Limine"

Low Term
See "Sentencing"

Mandamus
See "Petition"

Mandate
See "Petition"

Malice
See "Mental State"

Marsden Motion

A Marsden Motion is a request to replace the defendant's attorney with a different attorney. Unless there are unusual circumstances, it is usually a bad idea to bring a Marsden Motion.

Mental State

It is not enough that a defendant commit an act, he must also have a certain mental state before he can be convicted of a crime. The common mental states are General Intent, Specific Intent, and Malice.

For General Intent, the prosecution must prove that the defendant acted willfully. For Specific Intent the prosecution must prove that the defendant acted willfully and with the specific intent that the crime be committed. For Malice, the prosecution must prove that the defendant acted deliberately with conscious disregard for life.

Mid Term
See "Sentencing"

Motion

A Motion is a request that the court issue an order. As examples, "defendant moves that the Court continue the Trial date" means the defendant requests that the judge set a new date for the trial. "Defendant moves the Court for a discovery order," means the defendant requests that the judge order the District Attorney to give the defendant evidence concerning the case. The attorney "moves" the court to take some action. This process is known as a "motion."

Move
See "Motion"

Objection

A complaint to the court that something is being done wrong. As examples, if the prosecution vouches for a witness, the defense may state, "Objection – vouching." If the defense begins to argue with a witness, the prosecution may state, "Objection – argumentative."

When an objection is made, the court will rule either "overruled" or "sustained." Overruled means the court does not find the complaint valid. Sustained means that the court does find the complaint valid.

Own Recognizance

The release of defendant from jail without paying bail based on the defendant's promise to appear in court when required.

Party

Party refers to the plaintiff and the defendant in a case. In a California criminal matter, the "People of the State of California" are the plaintiff and they are represented by the District Attorney. The "People of the State of California" are a Party, and the defendant is a Party.

With few exceptions, only the attorney for a Party may file motions or other pleadings in a case. For example, the alleged victim is not a Party. The alleged victim cannot dismiss the case or even bring motions because he is not a Party.

Petition

A Petition, like a motion, is a request that the court issue an order. Petitions, however, are generally ruled on without a hearing and are often not directed to the trial court, but instead are directed to a reviewing court. The attorney "petitions" the court to take some action and the court issues a "writ" to cause the action to happen. The following are some of the more common petitions.

Petition for Writ of Habeas Corpus – see "Habeas Corpus."

Petition for Writ of Mandamus or Petition for Writ of Mandate is a petition asking a higher court to order the trial court to do something, such as mandate that the trial court grant a certain number of custody credits to a defendant.

Petition for Writ of Prohibition is a petition asking a higher court to order the trial court to stop doing something, such as prohibit the trial court from prosecuting the defendant.

Petition to Dismiss is a petition asking the court to dismiss a misdemeanor or a low level felony after the defendant has completed all of the terms of their sentence.

Preliminary Examination

A formal examination establish whether the prosecution has enough evidence to establish that a crime has been committed and that it was the defendant who committed the crime. Most hearsay is allowed, and the prosecution does not have to prove their case beyond a reasonable doubt. The prosecution only needs to convince a judge that the allegations in the Complaint are probably true. Sometimes called a Preliminary Hearing.

Preliminary Hearing Setting Conference
See "Conference"

Pre-Preliminary Hearing
See "Conference"

Pretrial Conference
See "Conference"

Prior

A prior conviction. The term usually refers to a prior conviction that can be used to give a defendant a longer sentence, such as a "strike" or a prior involving a prison term.

Prohibition
See "Petition"

Readiness
See "Conference"

Removal

An order directed to a warden or sheriff requiring a prisoner to be removed from that person's custody and taken to court to be a witness.

Romero Motion

A request that the court dismiss sentencing enhancements and give the defendant a lesser sentence.

Sentencing

Entry of an order giving the punishment the defendant will receive. California uses a three level sentence for felonies. A felony prison sentence will be expressed as three levels, such as 2,3,5 - the lower term, the middle term, and the upper term. If the defendant receives the lower term, he will be sentenced to two years plus any enhancements for prior "strike" offenses, prior prison terms, gang enhancements, gun enhancements, etc.

Side Bar

To have a conversation with the judge outside the presence of the jury while the jury is still in the room.

Status Conference

See "Conference"

Strike

Strike is generally given one of two meanings:
1. Erase, such as "strike Count One," meaning the defendant will no longer be charged with count one.
2. A serious or violent felony, such as "defendant suffers a strike for a robbery," meaning that defendant was previously convicted of robbery and that conviction will be used to enhance his current sentence if he is convicted.

Subpoena

An order telling a person that they must come to court to testify or produce evidence.

Suppress

To forbid the use of evidence. Example: defendant's house was searched without permission and without a warrant. If the court suppresses what was found, it cannot be used at trial and the prosecution is not even allowed to mention it.

Time Waiver

A defendant has the right to a speedy trial. A time waiver is an agreement that a certain amount of time will not be counted towards the time within which the case must be brought to trial.

Trial

The formal presentation of evidence against defendant.

Trial Setting Conference
See "Conference"

Trier of Fact

The person or group of persons who decide whether the defendant is guilty or not guilty. The trier of fact may be the jury, but some defendants opt for a court trial (also known as a bench trial) where the judge alone is the trier of fact.

Upper Term
See "Sentencing"

Voir Dire

Questioning of prospective jurors or experts regarding their eligibility to participate in a case.

West Plea

A plea entered so the defendant can get the benefits of a specific plea bargain, but not admit the conduct that the pled-to charge alleges. The plea is sometimes used for a defendant who claims actual innocence, but enters a plea to avoid the dangers of trial. Named after the case of *People v. West* (1970) 3 Cal. 3rd 595.

Wobbler

A charge that can be filed as a felony or a misdemeanor.

Writ
See "Petition"

D. ANSWERS TO BAIL QUESTIONS

1. What is bail?

Bail is the court's security to ensure that a defendant will appear at future court dates. It is a fixed amount that the court requires from a person before releasing that person from jail.

The bail can be as small as a promise to appear; it can be as high as several million dollars, or bail can be denied completely for a defendant facing very serious charges or a defendant who has previously failed to appear.

Bail may be in the form of a promise (known as an "own recognizance" or "OR" release), cash, real estate, bail bond, or other surety acceptable to the court.

2. Do I have to post bail if I can prove I am innocent?

Nearly everyone has heard "innocent until proven guilty," but this, unfortunately, does not apply when it comes to bail. A defendant may have a perfect alibi and absolute proof of innocence, but the court will generally not consider the strength of the prosecution's case when setting bail. Bail is initially set based primarily on the charges against the defendant, regardless of weaknesses in the case.

3. Can the amount of bail be reduced?

The court can reduce or increase bail upon the request of the defendant or the prosecution. When requesting a reduction, it is helpful for the defendant to show that he has strong ties to the community, such as home ownership, multiple family members in the area, long-term employment, and involvement in the community. However, when a bail reduction is requested, there is always the danger that bail will be increased instead of decreased.

4. What does the court consider when setting bail?

In setting, reducing, or denying bail, a judge or magistrate will take into consideration the protection of the public, the seriousness of the offense charged, the previous criminal record of the defendant, and the probability of the defendant appearing when ordered to do so. The court may also consider factor such as other outstanding warrants against the defendant, prior incidents where the defendant failed to make a court appearance, the criminal record of the defendant, the location and type of defendant's residence (owner or renter), the defendant's wealth, the amount of the defendant's gain from the crime charged, and the number of separate offenses charged.

Defendant's status as a homeowner in the area may be given great weight because it shows that defendant has a strong tie to the community and a strong reason to remain in the community.

The fact that the defendant has or has not asked for a jury trial may not be considered in fixing the amount of bail.

5. What is cash bail?

Cash bail means that the defendant deposits with the court (or the sheriff) the full amount of bail in cash. For example, if bail is set at $100,000, the defendant must post the full $100,000 with the court to be released on cash bail.

6. What is a real estate bond?

The court may accept real estate in lieu of bail, but the process may be difficult, time-consuming, and expensive. The person attempting to post real estate in lieu of bail must prove to the court that the equity in the real estate is at least twice the amount of the bail. This generally requires an appraisal of the property as well as title insurance to prove the amount of loans against the property. It is not enough that a person owns a house; the person must show that the value of the house less the value of any encumbrances on the house (loans, liens, judgments, etc.) is at least double the amount of bail.

For example, say bail is set at $100,000 and the defendant owns a house that he bought for $250,000, but still owes $50,000 on the house. If the house is appraised for $240,000, the defendant cannot bail out using the real estate because $240,000 less the $50,000 loan is $190,000, and that amount is not double the amount of the bond. House values fluctuate, and appraisers may give conservatively low values when making an appraisal for the court, so it is common for defendants to be surprised that the value of the family home falls far short of the amount required for release from custody.

A defendant is entitled to a hearing to determine the value of the equity in the real estate, and witnesses may be called at the hearing. This process may take a week, a month, or more depending on how long it takes to get the property appraised and get the proper documentation. However, even after obtaining the necessary documents and witnesses, unless the court is satisfied that the value of the equity is equal to twice the amount of the bail, release on real estate bond will be denied.

7. What is a bail bond?

A Bail Bond is a contract with a bail bondsman whereby the bondsman will guarantee to the court that the defendant will make all court appearances after his release on bail. If the defendant fails to go to court, the court will demand full payment of the bond from the bondsman.

8. How much does a bail bond cost?

The law generally sets the price of a bail bond at ten percent of the bail amount. For example, if the bail is set at $100,000 then the bail bond will cost $10,000. Some bondsmen are able to offer premium reductions for defendants that employ a private attorney, are past or present members of the military, are senior citizens or are union members. Combined discounts may reduce the bail amount by as much as 30%. For example, if the bail is set at $100,000 and the defendant is a past member of the military who hires a private attorney, the bond could cost $7,000 ($10,000 less $3,000 premium discount).

9. What is a bail source hearing?

Penal Code §1275.1(a) requires that bail cannot be accepted unless the court is convinced that no portion of the bail was feloniously obtained. This means that if the court believes part of the money used for bail came from criminal activity, bail will not be allowed.

If the prosecution believes that some or all of the bail money came from criminal activity, he must file a declaration that gives the court probable cause to believe that the source of the bail was feloniously obtained. The defendant is entitled to receive a copy of the declaration and then the defendant bears the burden of proving by a preponderance of the evidence that the source of the bail money was not criminal activity.

At the hearing, any person who can provide relevant testimony about the source of funds should be present, and the person posting bail (or paying the premium for a bail bond) should be prepared to provide financial documents to prove the source of bail, such as pay stubs, bank statements, tax returns, real estate deeds, and credit card statements.

If the defendant is able to prove the source of funds, bail must be accepted and he must be released.

10. When do I get bail back?

If the defendant has posted cash bond and then makes all necessary appearances in court, bail will be returned after defendant is sentenced and begins serving the sentence. If the defendant has posted a real estate bond, it will be exonerated – the lien against the real estate will be released.

11. Do I get back the money I paid for a bail bond?

No. The premium paid for a bail bond is not returned even if the case is dismissed or the defendant makes every required appearance in court. The amount paid for a bail bond is much like the amount paid for insurance on a car - the amount paid for car insurance is not returned just because the driver does not have any accidents. A bail bond is insurance that a defendant will appear in court when required, and the amount paid for the bond is not returned just because the defendant does appear.

12. What do I get back from the bondsman?

The bondsman keeps the money paid for the bond and will continue to collect payments towards any balance owed, but if you pledged any collateral to secure the bail bond, such as a deed to real estate or the pink slip to a vehicle, you get your collateral back after the case is over and the bail bond premium is fully paid.

13. What is a cosigner responsible for?

Cosigners are responsible for paying the bail bond premium if the defendant does not. Also, if the defendant does not appear in court as required, the cosigners is responsible for any financial losses to the bondsman as a result of the failure to appear.

∞◊∞◊∞

Thanks to Glen Pierce of Gotta Go Bail Bonds for answering the bail questions listed above. Glen can be reached at (661)633-2245 to answer additional questions.

E. ORDER OF HEARINGS

Terms are defined above. These short lists give the order in which hearings are conducted.

1. Felony

With few exceptions, the defendant must be present for all felony proceedings.

Court proceedings in Felony cases generally proceed as follows:
1. Arraignment on the Complaint
2. Conference (may be called Pre-Preliminary Hearing, Preliminary Hearing Setting Conference, Scheduling Conference, etc. This step may repeat many times.)
3. Preliminary Hearing
4. Arraignment on the Information
5. Pretrial Motions (this step may repeat many times)
6. Readiness Conference (this step may repeat many times)
7. Trial
8. Sentencing

2. Misdemeanor

For some misdemeanor proceedings, the attorney may be allowed to appear without the defendant being present.

Court proceedings in Misdemeanor cases generally proceed as follows:
1. Arraignment on the Complaint
2. Pretrial Motions (this step may repeat many times)
3. Pretrial Conference (this step may repeat many times)
4. Trial
5. Sentencing

F. HELP YOUR ATTORNEY

1. Introduction

Not every criminal defense attorney is bad, and not all of these generalizations apply to every attorney, but odds are your attorney suffers from one or more of these problems.

If you come to understand some of your attorney's problems, you may be in a better position to help your attorney help you.

a. Your attorney has too many cases.

Even the United States Attorney General has acknowledged that "Too often, defenders carry huge caseloads that make it difficult, if not impossible, for them to fulfill their legal and ethical responsibilities to their clients. Lawyers buried under these caseloads often can't interview their clients properly, file appropriate motions, conduct fact investigations, or spare the time needed to ask and apply for additional grant funding."[1]

As an example, "The American Bar Association and the National Advisory Commission on Criminal Justice Standards and Goals recommends caseload caps at 150 felony cases or 400 misdemeanor cases per full time attorney. But the 60 public defenders on Fresno's staff carry caseloads of more than four times that amount."[2]

According to the American Constitution Society, at least one public defender's office spent on average less than one hour per defendant, and the average caseload at another public defender's office was 2,225

---

[1] Attorney General Eric Holder February 18, 2010 speech. Available at https://www.justice.gov/opa/speech/attorney-general-eric-holder-addresses-department-justice-national-symposium-indigent
[2] *Can a Public Defender Really Handle 700 Cases a Year?*, Gabrielle Canon, July 27, 2015, available at http://www.motherjones.com/politics/2015/07/aclu-lawsuit-public-defense-fresno-california

misdemeanors per attorney per year.[3] These attorneys are clearly grossly overworked.

b. Your attorney is poor.

The Attorney General has also acknowledged that "When lawyers are provided to the poor, too often they cannot represent their clients properly due to insufficient resources... public defender programs are too many times under-funded."[4]

A subscription to a major legal search engine, such as Westlaw or LexisNexis, can cost $300 or more per year per user. A book of sample pleadings can cost more than a $1,000 per year. Most, if not all, public defender offices have access to these essential resources, but the cost of these necessities is simply too much for many criminal defense practitioners. Even if the resources are available to public defenders, through a local law library, or through another source, a heavy caseload (as described above) may prevent the attorney from having time to use these essential tools.

Further, an attorney is not the only member of a criminal defense team. An effective defense may require an investigator, a paralegal, and a myriad of scientific experts in fields such as DNA, fingerprint analysis, blood alcohol testing, ballistics, or accident reconstruction. Support personnel expect to be paid, but sometimes there simply isn't money for them, so the case proceeds without the necessary support staff.

c. Your attorney is inexperienced.

Every attorney has a first case. Should it be yours? It would be best if a new attorney were allowed to assist an experienced attorney on multiple trials before being thrown into the fray and defending his

---

[3] *When Excessive Public Defender Workloads Violate the Sixth Amendment Right to Counsel Without a Showing of Prejudice*, Laurence A. Benner, March 2011, American Constitution Society for Law and Policy
[4] *Holder* speech, supra.

client alone, but this is often not done. Sometimes a person will graduate law school, pass the bar, and find themselves to be an attorney, standing in front of a jury, defending their client against a veteran prosecutor, without having previously even sat through a trial.

d. Your attorney has personal problems.

Many attorneys are overworked, underpaid, and constantly under stress. Their everyday decisions can lead to other people spending a lifetime in jail, losing their children, or even being executed. It is a high-stress job which has led to a large number of attorneys having personal and family problems and a large number of attorneys turning to alcohol or drugs to cope. The problem is so widespread that there is an organization completely dedicated to the problem.

"The Other Bar is a network of recovering lawyers, law students and judges throughout the state, dedicated to assisting others within the legal profession who are suffering from alcohol and substance abuse problems. We are a private, non-profit corporation. Our organization is founded on the principle of anonymity and provides services in strict confidentiality. The program is voluntary and open to all California lawyers, judges and law students." (www.otherbar.org)

∞◊∞◊∞

Larry's Law – Don't show off for other inmates.

Your attorney, whether you hired him or her, whether you receive the Public Defender or were appointed a "street" lawyer, must have your confidence. Look out for the danger signs above but second guessing or grandstanding to perform for other inmates will only hurt your case.

~Larry Fields,
Attorney at Law
(661)861-9750

2. Don't sabotage your defense

Don't walk, don't talk, don't write, don't fight.

Don't Walk

When you have a scheduled court hearing, show up and be on time. Too often a defendant will post bail, forget to come to court, and end up getting another charge added – failure to appear.

For those who do not post bail, escape is sometimes easy – an inmate is allowed to simply walk away. An injured inmate may be taken to the hospital for treatment. If the inmate is not facing serious charges, he may be left alone with medical staff. The temptation is great to walk away, but this could result in an additional charge – escape.

Be where you are supposed to be when you are supposed to be there.

Don't Talk

The most common way defendants sabotage their defense is by talking.

Don't talk to your family or friends about the case or anyone involved in the case. Most jail calls are recorded. Concerned family and friends naturally ask a defendant about the case. The answers are often played in court and used to convict. Defendants often ask family members to contact the victim and attempt to reconcile. This can lead to an additional charge for witness intimidation.

Some defendants try to trick guards by talking in coded messages, trading phones with another inmate, or using another inmate's phone codes. The recordings of these calls are even more damning because the jury hears not only incriminating statements made during the call, but also that the defendant was trying to hide his actions.

Some defendants talk to other inmates about their cases. Often fellow inmates strike a deal to testify against one another in exchange for leniency. The jails are full of snitches.

To quote Attorney Bill Slocumb, "If you've been arrested, STFU." This appears to be an odd spelling of Shut Up.

Don't Write

Letters sent from jail are subject to search. Notes passed to other inmates can be intercepted or the inmate may give a note to a guard in hopes of gaining favoritism. These letters and notes are often used against the defendant.

Out-of-custody defendants have been known to chat about their case on Facebook or other social media. Some have even posted photographs of themselves with known gang members throwing gang signs. Such antics can destroy a defense or lead to additional charges.

Don't Fight

Jail is hard. Some inmates have little to lose because they have already been convicted and are awaiting transfer to prison where they will spend the rest of their life. If they attack a fellow inmate, it may raise their prestige. Fighting is rampant in jails and prisons.

If an inmate is already serving a life sentence, the prosecution often doesn't bother filing charges against the inmate. However, a defendant facing a short sentence may find himself facing a very long sentence if he is charged for a jail fight.

3. Cooperate with your defense team

Odds are, you know more about your case today than your attorney will ever know. You probably know your best defenses, and you probably have a pretty good idea about how to get in touch with witnesses that might help your case. If you are sitting in jail, you probably have some pretty good ideas about who might post bail, who might help with security for bail, and who might give you good character references to help secure a lower bail.

You can talk to your attorney about all of these things, but the odds are he either won't listen or he will forget something important. Your attorney will never care about your case as much as you do, but you can make him care more by putting your thoughts in writing and letting your attorney know that you've kept a copy of what you've written.

If you put something in writing, your attorney will almost always respond. If he does not respond, he runs the risk of being admonished by the court or the bar for failing to do so.

Any letter to your attorney should be short and to the point. The letter should be neatly printed and it should not contain gang symbols or characters, such as crossed out letters. It should not contain threats or harsh accusations. A long letter that is difficult to read will probably be considered unreadable and receive little attention. Letters to your legal team should be designed to get a favorable response, not to vent your anger about an unfair system.

Don't keep secrets from your defense team. If you know that your DNA will be on a piece of incriminating evidence, let your attorney know. If you know that your fingerprints will be at the crime scene, let your attorney know. If you know you are going to be seen on incriminating video recordings, let your attorney know.

You don't want your defense team to collect evidence that will harm your case, but if they don't know where the bad evidence is, they may accidently uncover it while looking for good evidence.

Several sample letters are found in this book in the section entitled "Sample Letters."

∞◊∞◊∞

Larry's Law – Sometimes the best thing to do is leave things alone.

If defending yourself was easy, everyone would do it and we wouldn't need attorneys. But defending a criminal case is rarely as easy as it appears from the outside looking in. Clients often think that every little aspect of a case needs to be put forward, but sometimes allowing seemingly beneficial evidence only gives the prosecution the opportunity to present negative evidence that otherwise would have been kept out. A skilled attorney knows these nuances and can guide your defense in the right direction even though you may not know or understand it. An experienced, professional criminal defense attorney knows the lay of the land: the cops that investigated your case, the prosecutors and the judges. He or she knows how to direct your defense in the right direction through motions and evidence.....experience pays, and so does your patience to let your attorney guide your case.

~Larry Fields,
Attorney at Law
(661)861-9750

G. REPLACE YOUR ATTORNEY

1. Introduction

Replacing your appointed attorney is often a bad idea. Many appointed attorneys, such as public defenders, are highly skilled and have years of trial experience. If you fire your attorney, it will usually cause delays, and judges are often against it. The most common ways to replace your attorney are listed here in order of best to worst.

2. Hire a different attorney

The services of an attorney are sometimes expensive because of the tremendous cost of becoming an attorney and the high cost of running a law practice.

Law books are expensive. As examples, *California Procedure* by Witkin currently retails for $829 and *California Three Strikes Sentencing* by the Rutter Group currently retails for $349. In addition to law books, most criminal defense practitioners also have to pay for online legal research tools, office space, support staff, computers, copy machines, and other items required to properly defend their clients.

This does not mean that a private attorney can't be affordable. Family and friends are often willing to assist with financing, and some attorneys take payment plans.

3. Ask your attorney to declare a conflict

If you want to get rid of your attorney, the odds are that the relationship just isn't working and he wants to get rid of you also. The attorney may be perfectly competent, but the two of you may have conflicting personalities or you may just have different ideas about how to proceed with the defense. Explain this to your attorney, and ask your attorney to declare a conflict so that another attorney will be appointed. A sample request letter is found in the section entitled Sample Letters.

4. Ask the court to give you a new attorney

You can ask the court to appoint a new attorney for you by filing a Marsden Motion (see the sample motion). The motion alleges that your attorney is incompetent or that he has a conflict of interest that cannot be reconciled.

The most likely outcome of a Marsden Motion is that you will lose.

If the motion is denied, your attorney will be mad at you and won't particularly want your case to turn out well. It is simple human nature – if someone attacks you, you don't want things to go well for that person.

If your motion is granted, the case will be assigned to a new attorney. The person making the assignments may also be mad at you – he won't want your case to turn out well. He gave you an attorney who he believed was appropriate, but you fired that attorney. He could replace the fired attorney with the best attorney available or he could assign your case to someone else – perhaps the assignment will be to the attorney he thinks is the least qualified.

5. Represent Yourself

A criminal defendant has the right to represent himself in court, but this is almost always a bad idea. Even attorneys who are trained in the law hire other attorneys to represent them because an attorney cannot effectively represent himself. You cannot effectively represent yourself either.

If your attorney is failing you and you can't get him to effectively represent you, tell the court. Get a new attorney, but don't try to be your own attorney.

∞◊∞◊∞

A person with a tumor may operate on his own skull. In America, people are free to do things, no matter how stupid, even represent themselves in a criminal case.

According to *Patterns and Trends in Federal Pro Se Defense, 1996-2011: an Exploratory Study*, Federal Courts Law Review, Vol 8, Issue 3 ©2015, "When going to trial (bench or jury), pro se defendants (15%) were more likely to be found guilty than defendants with retained (5%) or appointed counsel (3%)."

That is to say, pro per defendants were convicted three times as often as defendants with retained counsel and five times as often as defendants with appointed counsel.

The study also debunks the common myth that public defenders are not qualified. In this study, the appointed attorneys had a significantly higher acquittal rate.

H. IMMIGRATION CONSEQUENCES

1. General Deportation Rules

A defendant who is not a citizen of the United States should consider the immigration consequences of a conviction before entering a plea. An undocumented alien may be deported with or without reason, so any conviction could increase the chances of deportation, but even then, certain defenses to deportation exist which may even grant lawful permanent resident status. Resident aliens will generally only be deported for good cause, and certain criminal convictions may provide that good cause while others may have no effect at all, making it essential resident aliens know the exact immigration consequences of any crime they are accused of.

The specific immigration consequences of criminal history, whether for an undocumented alien or a lawful permanent resident are often difficult to determine, with many exceptions and only a few general rules. The result is that even experienced criminal defense attorneys often inadvertently place their non-citizen clients in danger of deportation when even subtle changes to the wording of a plea or in some cases pleading to a similar charge can avoid deportability completely. The complexity of immigration law and the severe consequences of getting it wrong, such as lifetime deportation and family separation makes it extremely dangerous for anyone who is not a United States citizen to enter into any guilty or no contest plea without first consulting an experienced immigration attorney first.

The list of non-citizens subject to deportation is found in *8 USC §1227*. The list includes many reasons not generally applicable to the average criminal defendant, such as deportation for becoming a public charge, plotting to overthrow the government, or falsification of immigration documents. Some crimes, such as recruiting child soldiers and participating in Nazi persecution, are deportable offenses, but the crimes are rarely charged today. The primary classifications of crimes that make noncitizens subject to deportation today are found in *8 USC §1227(a)(2)*:

(a) Classes of deportable aliens
Any alien (including an alien crewman) in and admitted to the United States shall, upon the order of the Attorney General, be removed if the alien is within one or more of the following classes of deportable aliens:...
(1) Criminal offenses

(A) General crimes
  (i) Crimes of moral turpitude
    Any alien who—
        (I) is convicted of a crime involving moral turpitude committed within five years (or 10 years in the case of an alien provided lawful permanent resident status under section 1255(j) of this title) after the date of admission, and
        (II) is convicted of a crime for which a sentence of one year or longer may be imposed,
      is deportable.
  (ii) Multiple criminal convictions
    Any alien who at any time after admission is convicted of two or more crimes involving moral turpitude, not arising out of a single scheme of criminal misconduct, regardless of whether confined therefor and regardless of whether the convictions were in a single trial, is deportable.
  (iii) Aggravated felony
    Any alien who is convicted of an aggravated felony at any time after admission is deportable.
  (iv) High speed flight
    Any alien who is convicted of a violation of section 758 of Title 18 (relating to high speed flight from an immigration checkpoint) is deportable.
  (v) Failure to register as a sex offender
    Any alien who is convicted under section 2250 of Title 18 is deportable.
  (vi) Waiver authorized
    Clauses (i), (ii), (iii), and (iv) shall not apply in the case of an alien with respect to a criminal conviction if the alien subsequent to the criminal conviction has been granted a full and unconditional pardon by the President of the United States or by the Governor of any of the several States.
(B) Controlled substances
  (i) Conviction
    Any alien who at any time after admission has been convicted of a violation of (or a conspiracy or attempt to violate) any law or regulation of a State, the United States, or a foreign country relating to a controlled substance (as defined in section 802 of Title 21), other than a single offense involving possession for one's own use of 30 grams or less of marijuana, is deportable.
  (ii) Drug abusers and addicts
    Any alien who is, or at any time after admission has been, a

drug abuser or addict is deportable.
(C) Certain firearm offenses
Any alien who at any time after admission is convicted under any law of purchasing, selling, offering for sale, exchanging, using, owning, possessing, or carrying, or of attempting or conspiring to purchase, sell, offer for sale, exchange, use, own, possess, or carry, any weapon, part, or accessory which is a firearm or destructive device (as defined in section 921(a) of Title 18) in violation of any law is deportable.
(D) Miscellaneous crimes
Any alien who at any time has been convicted (the judgment on such conviction becoming final) of, or has been so convicted of a conspiracy or attempt to violate-
  (i) any offense under chapter 37 (relating to espionage), chapter 105 (relating to sabotage), or chapter 115 (relating to treason and sedition) of Title 18 for which a term of imprisonment of five or more years may be imposed;
  (ii) any offense under section 871 or 960 of Title 18;
  (iii) a violation of any provision of the Military Selective Service Act (50 U.S.C. App. 451 et seq.) [now 50 U.S.C.A.§ 3801 et seq.] or the Trading With the Enemy Act (50 U.S.C. App. 1 et seq.) [now 50 U.S.C.A. § 4301 et seq.]; or
  (iv) a violation of section 1185 or 1328 of this title,
    is deportable.
(E) Crimes of domestic violence, stalking, or violation of protection order, crimes against children and
  (i) Domestic violence, stalking, and child abuse
  Any alien who at any time after admission is convicted of a crime of domestic violence, a crime of stalking, or a crime of child abuse, child neglect, or child abandonment is deportable. For purposes of this clause, the term "crime of domestic violence" means any crime of violence (as defined in section 16 of Title 18) against a person committed by a current or former spouse of the person, by an individual with whom the person shares a child in common, by an individual who is cohabiting with or has cohabited with the person as a spouse, by an individual similarly situated to a spouse of the person under the domestic or family violence laws of the jurisdiction where the offense occurs, or by any other individual against a person who is protected from that individual's acts under the domestic or family violence laws of the United States or any State, Indian tribal government, or unit of local government.
  (ii) Violators of protection orders

Any alien who at any time after admission is enjoined under a protection order issued by a court and whom the court determines has engaged in conduct that violates the portion of a protection order that involves protection against credible threats of violence, repeated harassment, or bodily injury to the person or persons for whom the protection order was issued is deportable. For purposes of this clause, the term "protection order" means any injunction issued for the purpose of preventing violent or threatening acts of domestic violence, including temporary or final orders issued by civil or criminal courts (other than support or child custody orders or provisions) whether obtained by filing an independent action or as a pendente lite order in another proceeding.

(F) Trafficking

Any alien described in section 1182(a)(2)(H) of this title is deportable....

2. **Aggravated Felony**

8 USC §1227(a)(2)(A)(iii) relates to Aggravated Felonies. A defendant convicted of an Aggravated Felony faces the worst possible immigration consequences because a defendant convicted of an Aggravated Felony is subject to deportation and will most likely be deported. Further, the defendant will generally be ineligible to apply for most forms of discretionary relief from deportation, such as voluntary departure or asylum. The general Aggravated Felony rules are that (1) the conviction be for a serious offense and that (2) the sentence be for a year or more, but not all offenses require a year sentence to be an Aggravated Felony.

In general, any conviction for theft, fraud, deceit or misrepresentation will be classified as an aggravated felony if the sentence is for 365 days or more OR if the loss was in excess of $10,000, or both. Any crime of violence with a sentence of 365 days or more is also an aggravated felony, as are certain specified crimes regardless of sentence such as possession of child pornography, felon in possession of a firearm and possession of a controlled substance for sale. A crime does not need to be a felony under the criminal law to be classified as an aggravated felony under the immigration law (e.g., misdemeanor possession for sale).

Aggravated felony classification can often be avoided through careful pleading, so make sure that you or your criminal defense counsel consult an experienced immigration attorney with knowledge of immigration-safe criminal pleading.

Aggravated Felonies are defined by *8 USC §1101(a)(43)* as follows:

(43) The term "aggravated felony" means—
    (A) murder, rape, or sexual abuse of a minor;
    (B) illicit trafficking in a controlled substance (as defined in section 802 of Title 21), including a drug trafficking crime (as defined in section 924(c) of Title 18);
    (C) illicit trafficking in firearms or destructive devices (as defined in section 921 of Title 18) or in explosive materials (as defined in section 841(c) of that title);
    (D) an offense described in section 1956 of Title 18 (relating to laundering of monetary instruments) or section 1957 of that title (relating to engaging in monetary transactions in property derived from specific unlawful activity) if the amount of the funds exceeded $10,000;
    (E) an offense described in—
      (i) section 842(h) or (i) of Title 18, or section 844(d), (e), (f), (g), (h), or (i) of that title (relating to explosive materials offenses);
      (ii) section 922(g)(1), (2), (3), (4), or (5), (j), (n), (o), (p), or (r) or 924(b) or (h) of Title 18 (relating to firearms offenses); or
      (iii) section 5861 of Title 26 (relating to firearms offenses);
    (F) a crime of violence (as defined in section 16 of Title 18, but not including a purely political offense) for which the term of imprisonment at least one year;
    (G) a theft offense (including receipt of stolen property) or burglary offense for which the term of imprisonment at least one year;
    (H) an offense described in section 875, 876, 877, or 1202 of Title 18 (relating to the demand for or receipt of ransom);
    (I) an offense described in section 2251, 2251A, or 2252 of Title 18 (relating to child pornography);
    (J) an offense described in section 1962 of Title 18 (relating to racketeer influenced corrupt organizations), or an offense described in section 1084 (if it is a second or subsequent offense) or 1955 of that title (relating to gambling offenses), for which a sentence of one year imprisonment or more may be imposed;
    (K) an offense that—
      (i) relates to the owning, controlling, managing, or supervising of a prostitution business;
      (ii) is described in section 2421, 2422, or 2423 of Title 18 (relating to transportation for the purpose of prostitution) if committed for commercial advantage; or

(iii) is described in any of sections 1581-1585 or 1588-1591 of Title 18 (relating to peonage, slavery, involuntary servitude, and trafficking in persons);
(L) an offense described in—
  (i) section 793 (relating to gathering or transmitting national defense information), 798 (relating to disclosure of classified information), 2153 (relating to sabotage) or 2381 or 2382 (relating to treason) of Title 18;
  (ii) section 3121 of Title 50 (relating to protecting the identity of undercover intelligence agents); or
  (iii) section 3121 of Title 50 (relating to protecting the identity of undercover agents);
(M) an offense that—
  (i) involves fraud or deceit in which the loss to the victim or victims exceeds $10,000; or
  (ii) is described in section 7201 of Title 26 (relating to tax evasion) in which the revenue loss to the Government exceeds $10,000;
(N) an offense described in paragraph (1)(A) or (2) of section 1324(a) of this title (relating to alien smuggling), except in the case of a first offense for which the alien has affirmatively shown that the alien committed the offense for the purpose of assisting, abetting, or aiding only the alien's spouse, child, or parent (and no other individual) to violate a provision of this chapter
(O) an offense described in section 1325(a) or 1326 of this title committed by an alien who was previously deported on the basis of a conviction for an offense described in another subparagraph of this paragraph;
(P) an offense (i) which either is falsely making, forging, counterfeiting, mutilating, or altering a passport or instrument in violation of section 1543 of Title 18 or is described in section 1546(a) of such title (relating to document fraud) and (ii) for which the term of imprisonment is at least 12 months, except in the case of a first offense for which the alien has affirmatively shown that the alien committed the offense for the purpose of assisting, abetting, or aiding only the alien's spouse, child, or parent (and no other individual) to violate a provision of this chapter;
(Q) an offense relating to a failure to appear by a defendant for service of sentence if the underlying offense is punishable by imprisonment for a term of 5 years or more;
(R) an offense relating to commercial bribery, counterfeiting, forgery, or trafficking in vehicles the identification numbers of which have been altered for which the term of imprisonment is at least one year;

(S) an offense relating to obstruction of justice, perjury or subornation of perjury, or bribery of a witness, for which the term of imprisonment is at least one year;
(T) an offense relating to a failure to appear before a court pursuant to a court order to answer to or dispose of a charge of a felony for which a sentence of 2 years' imprisonment or more may be imposed; and
(U) an attempt or conspiracy to commit an offense described in this paragraph.

The term applies to an offense described in this paragraph whether in violation of Federal or State law and applies to such an offense in violation of the law of a foreign country for which the term of imprisonment was completed within the previous 15 years. Notwithstanding any other provision of law (including any effective date), the term applies regardless of whether the conviction was entered before, on, or after September 30, 1996.

3. Crime of Violence

Conviction of a Crime of Violence may also trigger deportation. If the crime is committed against one's spouse or other form of domestic partner, the defendant is subject to deportation pursuant to *8 USC § 1227(a)(2)(E)*.

If the defendant receives a sentence of a year or more is imposed, the conviction becomes an Aggravated Felony even if the victim is not a domestic partner. Most crimes of violence are also Crimes of Moral Turpitude (see below), though there are immigration-safe plea options to many crimes of violence that if properly plead can cause only minor or possibly no immigration consequences. As always, make sure to consult an experienced immigration attorney before you enter a plea.

18 USC §16 defines Crime of Violence:

The term "crime of violence" means—
(a) an offense that has as an element the use, attempted use, or threatened use of physical force against the person or property of another, or
(b) any other offense that is a felony and that, by its nature, involves a substantial risk that physical force against the person or property of another may be used in the course of committing the offense.

This statutory definition may, however, be incorrect. A federal circuit court recently noted that the Due Process Clause precludes the government from taking away a person's life, liberty, or property under a statute so vague that it fails to give ordinary people fair notice of the conduct it punishes, or so without standard that it invites arbitrary enforcement. Based on this, the court found that the definition given above is void for vagueness under the Due Process Clause of the Fifth Amendment (*Baptiste v. Attorney General* (3rd Cir, November 8, 2016) 841 F.3rd 601). The United States Supreme Court is currently considering whether the statutory definition of Crime of Violence is valid (*Lynch v. Dimaya* (2016) 137 S.Ct. 31), but as of September 2017, the court has not yet decided. Therefore, a defendant who pleads to a crime of violence under the current definition may be subject to deportation.

4. Crime Involving Moral Turpitude

The term Crime Involving Moral Turpitude is difficult to define – so difficult that the courts have not even been able to do so. It generally means crimes that show a lack of good morals, such as theft crimes, intent to cause great bodily injury, crimes involving lewdness, and crimes involving malice.

A noncitizen may generally be deported if convicted a felony Crime Involving Moral Turpitude within five years of admission to the United States or if convicted of two felony Crimes Involving Moral Turpitude any time after entry.

There is also a little-understood waiver built into the immigration law that can eliminate the immigration consequences of a crime involving moral turpitude (CMT). This is known as the Petty Offense Exception, and applies when the sentence imposed on a misdemeanor CMT is less than six months and the maximum sentence possible is less than one year for aliens who were only convicted of a single CMT. The Petty Offense Exception even works for felony convictions reduced to a misdemeanor at a later date.

5. Controlled Substance Offense

A noncitizen may generally be deported if convicted of Controlled Substance Offense unless the offense is a single conviction of possession of marijuana less than 30 grams. Other that exception, any and all drug offenses render any alien subject to deportation. There is a defense available for certain drug convictions from 2011 and earlier, however any violation of probation or additional drug offenses will take away this defense. Other immigration-safe strategies for drug cases exist at plea, making it essential that you get expert immigration consequence advice prior to entering any guilty or no-contest plea to any drug charge, including misdemeanors and paraphernalia.

∞◊∞◊∞

The immigration section above was prepared by Immigration Attorney Andrew Fishkin. Mr. Fishkin served for ten years as a Senior Special Agent in the Immigration and Naturalization Service (INS) and following that agency's reorganization, continued to serve in the Department of Homeland Security, Bureau of Immigration and Customs Enforcement (ICE).

Why the change from enforcement to defense?

Andrew Fishkin was in charge of detaining human smugglers (Coyotes). On one occasion, he and his team had surrounded an apartment where the human traffickers had hidden a large group of undocumented immigrants. The officers had control of the situation and began to move the immigrants, who were cramped in the small room, onto a truck. However, there was one individual in the corner who wouldn't move. Agent Andrew Fishkin addressed the man in Spanish, "stand up."

The man only smiled, and when Agent Fishkin tried to physically move him, the man screamed in pain. Then, one of man's companions told the agent, "The Coyote broke his knees with a bat in front of everyone to see what would happen if they tried to flee."

Attorney Andrew Fishkin says, "that really got to me. Right then, I realized I was on the wrong side of law."

So he left the department, enrolled in law school, graduated, passed the state bar exam, and began to defend undocumented immigrants. Today, Andrew Fishkin is part of United States Army Reserve, actively helps the community, makes donations to local organizations, is a member of The Rotary Club, and says, "Whatever I give, I do so from the heart."

That's Attorney Andrew Fishkin, Immigration Defense Attorney focusing on Deportation/Removal Defense.

Mr. Fishkin can be reached through his webpage www.lawyerfish.com or by phone at (661)322-6776.

I. MOTIONS BEFORE TRIAL

1. Introduction

A motion is a request that the court issue an order. Motions before trial are those motions that make requests in preparation for trial. These motions are generally not heard by the judge who will preside over trial; instead, they are heard by a motions judge. Common motions, in roughly order of use, include:

1. Continuance – a request for more time to prepare for trial.
2. Discovery – a request that the Prosecution be ordered to give you evidence concerning your case.
3. Bail – a request that the court set bail or reduce bail to a reasonable level so that the defendant can post bail.
4. Lineup – a request that a witness view defendant as part of a lineup.
5. Suppress – a request that the court rule that evidence seized from you cannot be used against you at trial.
6. Set Aside the Information – a request that the court rule that the evidence presented at the preliminary hearing was insufficient to lead a person to believe that a crime was committed and that it was defendant who committed it.
7. Recall Warrant – request that the court recall an arrest warrant and set the case for further hearings.
8. Pitchess – a request that the court look in the personnel files of the officers involved in the prosecution to see if they have previously been accused of any misconduct that could be used against them at trial.
9. Withdraw Plea – a request that the court allow a defendant to withdraw his plea of guilty or no contest and enter a not guilty plea.
10. Prohibit Restrictions on Right to Counsel – a request that the court grant defendant free, unmonitored phone calls to his attorney.
11. Traverse – a request that the court first determine that the officer obtaining a search warrant misled the judge when obtaining the warrant and, second, rule that the evidence seized under the warrant cannot be used against you at trial.
12. Disclose Informant – a request that the court provide the defendant with the name and contact information for a confidential informant who gave law enforcement information concerning the case against defendant.
13. Unseal Affidavit (Hitch Motion) – a request that the court open the affidavit that was used to obtain a search warrant and give the defendant a copy of the affidavit.

14. Enforce Agreement – a request that the court order the prosecution to abide by the terms of any agreements.
15. Motion for Sanctions (Trombetta Motion) – a request that the court punish the prosecution for losing valuable evidence.
16. Dismiss for Speedy Trial Violation (Serna) – a request that the case be dismissed because trial, preliminary hearing, or other required proceedings were not held within the statutory time period.
17. Dismiss for Delay in Prosecution – a request that the case be dismissed because there has been undue delay in the prosecution.
18. Motion to Set Motions Date – some courts have a set date for hearing of motions and motions will only be heard on that date. This is a request that the court set a date for hearing of motions.
19. Joinder – a request that the court consider that pleadings filed by a codefendant also be applied to defendant.
20. Marsden Motion – a request that the court replace defendant's attorney with a different attorney.

2. Notice requirements

"Notice" simply means providing a copy of a motion to other interested parties. In most cases, this means giving a copy of your motion to the district attorney, but some motions must also be served on the probation department, a law enforcement agency, the city attorney, county counsel, or someone else.

Generally, a defendant cannot serve his own pleadings, and most law firms use a service, such as Attorney Messenger Service (661-324-8018), to serve pleadings. AMS picks up pleadings from the law firm, serves all required parties, files the pleadings with the court, and then returns endorsed copies to the law firm.

Service of motions on counsel for codefendants is technically not required for most motions, but local rules often require service on counsel for codefendants, so it is generally the best practice to always serve each attorney for each codefendant. It is easier to serve a motion on extra people than it is to enforce technical rules, so non-essential parties are shown in the chart. Service times refer to personal service, but the court may require an additional five days if service is by mail. The number of days refers to court days – days the court is in session.

The chart on the following page summarizes notice requirements and recommendations.

Motion	Who to Serve	Notice	Notes
General Rule	District Attorney	10 days	*Rule of Court 4.111*; Unless otherwise noted, motions require ten day notice
Pitchess (Discover Personnel Files)	District Attorney, Police Agency, and Agency's Attorney	16 days	*Code of Civil Procedure §1005(b)*, Service on DA is not technically required, but clerks may insist.
Suppress Evidence	District Attorney	10 days	*Penal Code §1538.5* Time is reduced to five days if the motion is brought before preliminary hearing.
Ex Parte	None	None	Applies to few motions – mostly requests for funds.
Continuance	District Attorney	2 days	Also serve the probation department if motion is brought after conviction
Expunge Conviction	District Attorney, Probation Department	15 days	*Penal Code §1203.4*
Declare Defendant Incompetent	District Attorney	None	*Penal Code §1367 or 1368*
Withdraw Plea	District Attorney, Probation Department	10 days	*Penal Code §1018.* Some courts do not require advance notice, but best practice is to serve and file at least ten day before hearing.
Substitute Attorney	District Attorney, Prior Attorney	None	Best practice is to file at least 2 days before hearing.
Strike Prior Convictions	District Attorney, Probation	2 days	Commonly known as a *Romero, Rule 4.437(a)*
Statement in Mitigation	District Attorney, Probation	4 days	*Rule 4.437(a)*
Return Property	District Attorney, the agency holding the property	3 days	*Code of Civil Procedure §1201.5*
Substitute Attorney	District Attorney	None	Best to give two days' notice

J. SAMPLE MOTIONS BEFORE TRIAL

Introduction

Most motions are fact specific to a particular case, so it is not possible to present "ready to file" or completely generic examples for each of these motions. Therefore, the motions presented here are, for the most part, gleaned from the files of the Superior Court in Kern County and are from real cases, with names and certain facts changed.

The motions offered here are examples of some of the common types of motions that may be filed, but this is only a short, cursory overview of the types of motions that may be heard by the court.

∞◊∞◊∞

Larry's Law – Watch the date, time, and location

Motions often have very technical rules that are difficult to comply with and vary from court to court. For example, in Kern County, criminal motions are heard on multiple different calendars on different days and times depending on the city, offense level, and whether the motion is brought before, during, or after preliminary hearings. In Bakersfield, misdemeanor motions are heard in Division LM on Tuesday through Thursday at 8:30 a.m., but felony motions are heard Monday through Friday in Department CC (some Divisions, some Departments). Motions requiring testimony are heard at 10:00 a.m., but other motions are heard at 8:30 a.m., unless it is a motion to continue, and then it is heard in Department One, but only Tuesday through Thursday, unless the motion is heard on the date of Readiness, then it can be heard on a Friday or if the motion is heard on the date of trial, then it can be heard on the Monday trial call calendar. Criminal motions in Delano, which is in the same county, are heard at 10:00 a.m. in Department A on Monday, but if the motion is heard on Thursday, it will be Department B...

Are you confused yet? The rules are so confusing that some attorneys and paralegals even have to check with the court clerks to ensure that they are setting the motion at the right time, on the right day, in the right department (or maybe division... maybe room?).

~Larry Fields,
Attorney at Law
(661)861-9750

1. Continuance

Note: A continuance is a request for more time to prepare. The motion asks the court to move a hearing that has already been set to a later date. A continuance is required in most cases that proceed to trial, and the defendant is usually required to "waive time" for a continuance.

Elliot Magnus
641 H Street
Bakersfield, CA 93304
(661)395-0240

Attorney for Dave Douglass

IN THE SUPERIOR COURT OF THE STATE OF CALIFORNIA,
IN AND FOR THE COUNTY OF KERN

People of the State of California,	CASE NO. 123456
Plaintiffs,	DEFENDANT'S MOTION TO CONTINUE TRIAL
- v. -	DATE: October 16, 2017
Dave Douglass,	TIME: 8:30 a.m.
	DEPT: 1
Defendant	Trial date: October 31, 2017
	Readiness date: October 30, 2017

TO THE COURT AND THE DISTRICT ATTORNEY:

PLEASE TAKE NOTICE that at the date and time indicated above, or as soon thereafter as the matter can be heard in the above entitled court, the defendant will move that the Court continue the Trial date.

The motion will be based on this notice of motion, the attached declaration, the memorandum of points and authorities served and filed herewith, the records on file in this action and on such oral and documentary evidence as may be presented at the hearing.
Dated:

By   Elliot Magnus,
Attorney for Dave Douglass

DECLARATION IN SUPPORT OF MOTION TO CONTINUE

I, Elliot Magnus, Attorney for Defendant, declare and aver as follows:

    Our investigator has been unable to locate a key witness, Wayne Whitt. Mr. Whitt is a percipient witness to the shooting herein. He is the only witness who is able to testify regarding the facts before, during, and after.

    Further, I received new discovery this week that will require investigation.

    Finally, the court appointed firearm expert for the defense has not completed or sent his final report to me.

    Based on the foregoing, I respectfully request a reasonable continuance in the above entitled matter.

Dated:

                                                               _____
                                       By   Elliot Magnus,
                                                   Attorney for Dave Douglass

∞◊∞◊∞

It takes time to prepare a case for trial, especially if the case involves serious charges or multiple defendants.

The attorney may, therefore, request multiple continuances, each of which will require the defendant to waive time. A defendant has the right to a speedy trial, but this right often conflicts with the defendant's right to effective assistance of counsel. An unprepared attorney may not be effective.

It is usually a good idea to waive time when requested by your attorney. While it might be possible to force a case to trial before the prosecution is ready, it is a risky strategy to force the case to trial when your own attorney is not ready. If you feel that the case is not progressing quickly, ask your attorney to explain delays in your case and what progress is being made.

Often, the attorney is also anxious to get a case to trial, but he has to request a continuance because some necessary witness is unavailable or some expert needs more time to do more testing.

POINTS, AUTHORITIES, AND ARGUMENT

Penal Code §1050(b) provides that:

> To continue any hearing in a criminal proceeding, including the trial, (1) a written notice shall be filed and served on all parties to the proceeding at least two court days before the hearing sought to be continued, together with affidavits or declarations detailing specific facts showing that a continuance is necessary....

The grant or denial of a motion for continuance is an act within the Court's discretion (*Ungar v. Sarafite* (1964) 376 US 575, 589), but this discretion is not without bounds:

> While the determination of whether in any given case a continuance should be granted normally rests in the discretion of the trial court, that discretion may not be exercised in such a manner as to deprive the defendant of a reasonable opportunity to prepare his defense. [citation]

In considering a request for a continuance, the Court must consider the defendant's right to a fair trial. (*People v. Courts* (1985) 37 Cal 3rd 784, 794)

The right to counsel (*United States Constitution, Amendment VI; California Constitution article I, section 15*) includes the right to adequately prepare a defense (*People v. Maddox* (1967) 67 Cal 2nd 647, 652).

The unavailability of a witness whose testimony has a legitimate tendency to prove or disprove a fact that could influence the decision in the case is good cause for a continuance. (See *People v. Dunstan* (1922) 59 Cal App 574, 584. See also *Owens v. Superior Court* (1980) 28 Cal 3rd 238, 250)

∞◊∞◊∞

Recent Favorable Supreme Court Fourth Amendment Cases

- *Georgia v. Randolph* (2006) 547 U.S. 103 (2006) - Police cannot conduct a warrantless search of a home if any one occupant objects.
- *United States v. Jones* (2012) 565 U.S. 400 – Police must obtain a warrant to attach a GPS device to a vehicle.
- *Riley v. California* (2014) 134 S.Ct. 2473 - Police must obtain a warrant to search a cell phone taken from a person who has been arrested.

2. Compel Discovery

Larry Fields
2112 17th St
Bakersfield, CA 93301
(661)861-9750

Attorney for Dave Douglass

IN THE SUPERIOR COURT OF THE STATE OF CALIFORNIA,
IN AND FOR THE COUNTY OF KERN

People of the State of California,	CASE NO. 123456
Plaintiffs,	MOTION TO COMPEL DISCOVERY
- v. -	[*Brady Motion, Penal Code §1054.5*]
	DATE: October 16, 2017
Dave Douglass,	TIME: 8:30 a.m.
	DEPT: CC
Defendant	Trial date: October 31, 2017
	Readiness date: October 30, 2017

TO THE COURT AND THE DISTRICT ATTORNEY:
PLEASE TAKE NOTICE that at the date and time indicated above, or as soon thereafter as the matter can be heard in the above entitled court, the defendant will move the Court for an order compelling discovery.

The motion will be made on the ground that the Deputy District Attorney or the Prosecution team has in their actual or constructive possession certain items of evidence which defense counsel is legally entitled to inspect; the defense has informally requested said evidence, but the District Attorney has not provided said evidence to the defense.

The motion will be based on this notice of motion, the attached declaration, the memorandum of points and authorities served and filed herewith, the records on file in this action and on such oral and documentary evidence as may be presented at the hearing.

Dated:

By Larry Fields,
Attorney for Dave Douglass

POINTS, AUTHORITIES, AND ARGUMENT

DUE PROCESS REQUIRES THE PROSECUTION TO PROVIDE DISCOVERY IN ORDER TO PROTECT DEFENDANT'S RIGHT TO PRESENT A DEFENSE AND RIGHT TO A FAIR TRIAL

"(T)he interest of the prosecution is not that it shall win the case, but that it shall bring forth the true facts surrounding the commission of the crime so that justice shall be done ..." (*Berger v. United States* (1934) 295 U.S. 78, 88)

The purpose of the discovery process in criminal cases is to guarantee a defendant a fair trial by giving him equal access to information so that he may be permitted to present all relevant evidence in his behalf. This aim was emphasized in *U.S. v. Nixon* (1974) 418 U.S. 683, 709, where the United States Supreme Court stated:

> We have elected to employ an adversary system of criminal justice in which the parties contest all issues before a court of law. The need to develop all relevant facts in the adversary system is both fundamental and comprehensive. The ends of criminal justice would be defeated if judgments were to be founded on a partial or speculative presentation of the facts. The very integrity of the judicial system and public confidence in the system depend on full disclosure of all the facts, within the framework of the rules of evidence. To ensure that justice is done, it is imperative to the function of courts that compulsory process be available for the production of evidence needed by the prosecution or by the defense.

The sources in expanding criminal discovery can be found in the "Due Process Clause" of the 5th and 14th Amendments to the United States Constitution, and in the 6th Amendment to the United States Constitution.

The United States Supreme Court also stated in *Nixon*, supra, that to vindicate these guarantees, the courts have a "manifest duty" to ensure that all relevant and admissible evidence be produced.(id.)

Brady v. Maryland (1963) 373 U.S. 83, and its progeny, explain that the prosecution violates a defendant's Due Process rights when it fails to disclose to the defendant prior to trial, "evidence favorable to an accused. . . where the evidence is material either to guilt or to punishment, irrespective of the good faith or bad faith of the prosecution." (id. at 87). This is the "Brady Rule."

The Brady Rule is not intended "to displace the adversary system as the primary means by which truth is uncovered, but to ensure that a miscarriage of justice does not occur" (*U.S. v. Bagley* (1985) 473 U.S. 667, 675). This limited departure from the adversary system "illustrates the special role played by the American prosecutor in the search for truth in criminal trials" (*Strickler v. Greene* (1999) 527 U.S. 263). The prosecutor's unique role "transcends that of an adversary: [the prosecutor] is the representative not of an ordinary party to a controversy, but of a sovereignty . . . whose interest . . . in a criminal prosecution is not that it shall win a case, but that justice shall be done.' " *Bagley*, supra at 675, fn.6 (quoting *Berger v. United States* (1935) 295 U.S. 78, 88; see also *Kyles v. Whitley* (1995) 514 U.S. 419, 437).

Due Process requires fundamental fairness in the prosecution of a criminal case (*Lisenba v. California* (1941) 314 U.S. 219, 236). Implicit in the concept of fundamental fairness is the idea that the defendant must have the opportunity to present a complete defense (*California v. Trombetta* (1984) 467 U.S. 479, 485). The prosecution can ensure that a defendant has the opportunity to present a complete defense by providing access to favorable evidence (*Brady, supra*).

The United States Supreme Court has held that "[s]uppression by the prosecution of evidence favorable to an accused who has requested it violates Due Process where the evidence is material either to guilt or to punishment, irrespective of the good faith or bad faith of the prosecution." (*Brady, supra*). It is the character of the evidence, rather than the character of the prosecutor, that determines whether the suppression of favorable evidence results in constitutional error (*U.S. v. Agurs* (1976) 427 U.S. 97, 110).

The proper inquiry where the question is whether the prosecution violated a defendant's right to Due Process by withholding evidence is:
(1) whether the evidence was favorable to the defendant; and,
(2) whether the evidence was material to guilt or punishment.
(See *United State v. Bagley* (1985) 473 U.S. 667).

For purposes of this analysis, it does not matter whether the evidence was suppressed by the prosecutor or by the other agents on the case (*Kyles v. Whitley* (1995) 514 U.S. 419). Rather, the question is whether the evidence was suppressed by the prosecution, for which both the prosecutors and the investigators serve as agents.(id.)

The ultimate responsibility for ensuring that exculpatory evidence is provided in accordance with Brady rests with the prosecutor (id. at 438). A miscommunication between the prosecutor and the investigators that results in the suppression of exculpatory evidence is no excuse for a Brady violation (id.). As the Supreme Court explained in *Kyles v. Whitley*, since "the prosecutor has the means to discharge the government's Brady responsibility if he will, any argument excusing a prosecutor from disclosing what he does not happen to know about boils down to a plea to substitute the police for the prosecutor, and even for the courts themselves, as the final arbiters of the government's obligation to ensure fair trials." (id.)

THE PROSECUTION'S DISCOVERY DUTY OF DISCLOSURE EXTENDS TO ALL MEMBERS OF THE PROSECUTION TEAM

The Prosecution has a duty to seek out and disclose all discoverable materials held by members of the "prosecution team."

The prosecutors assigned to try a case have the duty "to learn of any favorable evidence known to others acting on the government's behalf in the case" (*Kyles v. Whitley* (1995) 514 U.S. 419, 437). Accordingly, the Brady/Kyles rule extends to all members of the "prosecution team," which includes both investigative and prosecutorial personnel (*U.S. v. Morris* (7th Cir. 1996) 80 F. 3rd 1151, 1170 (citing with favor *Carey v. Duckworth* (7th Cir. 1984) 738 F. 2nd 875, 878, for proposition that prosecution team includes federal DEA agents and local police)).

The Prosecution is not required to review the files of agencies that have no involvement in the investigation or prosecution (*Morris, supra*), but prosecutors are required to examine the files of those entities who actively participate in the investigation or prosecution of a case (See *Kyles, supra*; *Morris*, supra at 1169).

It is well established that a prosecutor is deemed to have "control" over all members of an investigatory team and that evidence maintained by cooperating entities falls within the scope of the Prosecution's Brady obligation (*Kyles*, supra, at pp. 437-438 ("any favorable evidence known to the others acting on the government's behalf is imputed to the prosecution."; *U.S. v. Zuno-Arce* (9th Cir. 1995) 44 F. 3rd 1420 ("Exculpatory evidence cannot be kept out of the hands of the defense just because the prosecutor does not have it, where an investigating agency does.")

DEFENDANT SPECIFICALLY REQUESTS DISCLOSURE OF THE FOLLOWING EVIDENCE:

First. The date and nature of any felony or misdemeanor arrest or conviction of any participant in or witness to the alleged crime.

Penal Code §1054.1 provides for defense discovery of "felony convictions of material witnesses whose credibility is likely to be critical to the outcome of the trial." *Evidence Code §780* and *People v. Castro* (1985) 38 Cal 3rd 301, 211, allow impeachment of any witness by felony convictions involving "moral turpitude." Impeachment of any witness by prior conduct not amounting to a felony and involving "moral turpitude" is also proper. (*People v. Wheeler* (1992) 4 Cal 4th 284) Accordingly, records of arrests and convictions of witnesses for felonies and misdemeanors are discoverable, at least if the conduct involves "moral turpitude." (*People v. Santos* (1994) 30 Cal App 4th 169.)

In *Hill v. Superior Court of Los Angeles County* (1974) 10 Cal 3rd 812, 817, the California Supreme Court held that the felony conviction records and the records of arrests and detentions of prospective witnesses are discoverable by the defendant, upon a showing of good cause, for the purpose of impeachment.

Second. The names, addresses and telephone numbers of any and all persons who were percipient witnesses to the offense alleged, including all persons who were held in the same cell with Defendant at the time of his arrest and all persons present when Defendant was examined in any way.

Persons held in the same cell with Defendant at the time of his arrest may be able to testify as to his state of sobriety, his demeanor, any apparent injury he suffered, any statements he made, or any statements made to him by law enforcement. Such evidence may be used to impeach Prosecution witnesses.

Penal Code §1054.1(a) provides that the Prosecution must disclose the names and addresses of persons intended to be called as witnesses. No legitimate reason exists to withhold discovery of their telephone numbers, and inconvenience to the witnesses will result from unannounced contacts by a defense investigator. Additionally, *Penal Code §§841.5(c), 1054.2* implicitly recognize the right of defense counsel to obtain the telephone numbers of victims and witnesses.

Third. Any dispatch tapes relative to the incident within the subject matter of this action.

Tape recordings or records of radio transmissions concerning the facts underlying the charges against the defendant may be relevant to the credibility of witnesses and are therefore discoverable. (*United States v. Strifler* (9th Cir 1988) 851 F 2nd 1197; *Davis v. Alaska* (1974) 415 US 308.)

Tape recordings of radio and telephone calls to the police department and the times of police responses are public records within the meaning of *Government Code §6200* and may not be destroyed for at least two years (*80 Ops Atty Gen 908* (1981)).

Fourth. Any communication tapes between any officer and the communication center and between officers involved in the incident that is the subject matter of this action.

See authority under the Third request.

Fifth. Any calls to 911 or law enforcement concerning the subject matter of this action.

See authority under the Third request.

Sixth. Any documents including, but not limited to, curriculum vitaes, and written reports and/or notes for any expert witness the prosecution intends to call as a witness at trial.

Penal Code §1054.1(f), by implication, provides for defense discovery of identifying information regarding experts. In *People v. Johnson* (1974) 38 Cal App 3rd 228, the Court of Appeal stated:

> Where it is appropriate, the defendant may discover the reports of the state's experts concerning their examination of real evidence [citation omitted]; discovery of the identity of state experts is analogous.

Evidence that tends to impeach the reliability of the state's expert is "exculpatory evidence" which state was obligated to turn over to defendant. (*People v. Garcia* (1993) 17 Cal. App. 4th 1169).

Seventh. All real evidence seized or obtained as a part of the investigation of the offenses charged.

Penal Code §1054.1(c) provides for such discovery.

Eighth. All evidence, however stored, that any defendant, former defendant, person associated with any defendant or former defendant, or any witness in this matter was a gang member, associate of a gang, or in any way affiliated with a gang before the incident leading to the instant case.

Penal Code §1054.1(c) and (e) allow for such discovery. Defendant specifically requests:

All evidence, however stored, that Defendant, any codefendant, and any witness was a gang member, an associate of a gang, or in any way affiliated with a gang before the incident leading to the instant case.

All evidence, however stored, that any person identified in Defendant's Facebook or other social media account was a gang member, an associate of a gang, or in any way affiliated with a gang before the incident leading to the instant case.

All evidence, however stored, that Eastside Boys or that any member, associate or other person believed by law enforcement to be related to that group participates in any crime charged herein for the benefit of Eastside Boys.

Ninth. An opportunity to examine all demonstrative and real evidence, including charts, diagrams and other exhibits, whether obtained as part of the investigation of the offenses charged or not, that the Prosecution intends to offer in evidence at trial or to be viewed by the jury.

The Prosecution's duty to disclose includes trial exhibits because the defense must disclose defense trial exhibits to the prosecution *(Penal Code §1054.3(b); Izazaga v. Superior Court* (1991) 54 Cal. 3rd 356, 375).

Tenth. Any original notes taken by any police officer relating to the interview of any witness intended to be called by the District Attorney to testify against any defendant.

In *People v. Angeles* (1985) 172 Cal App 3rd 1203, the Court of Appeal stated, " '… [Law enforcement officers] must take reasonable precautions to preserve for trial [their] original handwritten notes made in the course of interrogating a criminal defendant unless the interrogation is tape recorded and the tape is preserved.' ..."

Due process requires disclosure of any evidence that may undermine the credibility or probative value of prosecution evidence. (*United States v. Strifler* (9th Cir 1988) 851 F 2nd 1197.)

Additionally, the original notes of police officers are reports and contain statements whose disclosure is required by *Penal Code §1054.1(f)*.

In *Funk v. Superior Court of Los Angeles County* (1959) 52 Cal 2nd 423, the court noted that the defendant "moved for an order directing that he be allowed to examine the original notes made by the officers and to inspect and copy written statements prepared from the notes... The showing made by petitioner is sufficient to entitle him to production of the documents he wishes to inspect. It is settled that, during trial, an accused can compel the People to produce written statements of prosecution witnesses relating to the matters covered in their testimony. [Citation omitted.] As recent decisions of this court illustrate, there is no sound basis for applying a different rule merely because production is requested prior to, rather than during trial."

Eleventh. Promises, offers, or inducements

The prosecutor has a duty to disclose any explicit promise, offer, or inducement extended to prosecution witnesses. In *U.S. v. Bagley* (1985) 473 U.S. 667, the Supreme Court found a *Brady* violation for a failure to disclose written contracts with informant witnesses. In *In re Sassounian* (1995) 9 Cal. 4th 535 the California Supreme Court concluded the prosecution withheld favorable evidence when it failed to disclose evidence of benefits provided, and promises made, to a jailhouse informant.

The prosecution has a duty to disclose any "implied promise," such as when the words are not expressed but the substance implies the witness will receive a benefit. In *Giglio v. U.S.* (1972) 405 U.S. 150, the Supreme Court found a Brady violation for the failure to disclose that a prosecution witness had been told to rely on the government's good judgment whether he would be prosecuted if he agreed to testify.

The prosecutor cannot evade the duty to disclose promises by extending such offers in secret to the witness' attorney (*People v. Phillips* (1985) 41 Cal. 3rd 29, 47; full disclosure of any agreement between the prosecution and a witness or the witness's attorney is required, regardless of whether the witness has been fully informed of the agreement).

Twelfth. Promises in prior cases

When a prosecution witness, who is currently facing prosecution, has received benefits to cooperate with law enforcement in prior cases, the prosecution has a duty to disclose this fact. In *People v. Kasim* (1997) 56 Cal. App. 4th 1360, 1382, a prosecution witness, currently facing prosecution, had received benefits in the past by cooperating with law enforcement and thus had reason to believe they would in the instant case. The court concluded this evidence must be disclosed because the jury "was entitled to know about all historical events bearing on these witnesses' propensity to be truthful or untruthful."

Thirteenth. Pending charges

In *People v. Coyer* (1983) 142 Cal. App. 3rd 839, 842, the court held that "a defendant is entitled to discovery of criminal charges currently pending against prosecution witnesses anywhere in the state" because "the pendency of criminal charges is material to a witness' motivation in testifying even when no express 'promise of leniency or immunity' have been made." This decision was reaffirmed in *People v. Hayes* (1992) 3 Cal. App. 4th 1238.

Fourteenth. Parole or probation status

In *Davis v. Alaska* (1974) 415 U.S. 308, 319, the United States Supreme Court held that a defendant has the right to prove at trial that a prosecution witness is on probation, in order to establish that the witness' testimony is biased.

In *People v. Price* (1991) 1 Cal. 4th 324, 486, the California Supreme Court held that a defendant is entitled to prove that a prosecution witness is on parole "to show the witness' potential bias resulting from concern about possible revocation."

Fifteenth. Drug or alcohol use

Evidence that a prosecution witness is addicted to, or affected by, alcohol or an illegal drug is admissible to impeach the credibility of that witness when there is evidence that the witness was under the influence of alcohol or another drug when the events occurred about which the witness would testify, or when the witness' mental faculties were actually impaired by the drug habit (*People v. Smith* (1970) 4 Cal. App. 3rd 403, 412; *People v.*

Hernandez (1976) 63 Cal. App. 3rd 393, 405.

Sixteenth. Training and certification records regarding the use and operation of any testing equipment for the person or persons who conducted any testing concerning any evidence related to this matter.

Presumably, testing equipment will not give accurate results if it is not properly operated. The qualifications of the persons performing the tests on seized items are discoverable for impeachment purposes and as being exculpatory (*Brady, supra, Penal Code §1054.1(e)*).

Seventeenth. Any photographs taken of the Defendant at or near the time of the Defendant's arrest on these charges.

Penal Code §1054.1(c) requires the prosecution to disclose real evidence obtained as part of the investigation of the offenses charged. This, obviously, includes any photographs the Prosecution team took of the Defendant.

Eighteenth. A listing of any codes, shorthand, messages, and acronyms used in any report, computer file, or other document used or prepared in the investigation of this case.

The codes are foundational information under *People v. Adams* (1976) 59 Cal App 3rd 559. Due process forbids the Prosecution from using codes to keep information from the Defense.

Nineteenth. Any evidence to be used in rebuttal of the defense case.

The identities and statements of witnesses whom the prosecution intends to call in rebuttal of the defense are discoverable. (*Izazaga v. Superior Court* (1991) 54 Cal 3rd 356)

The Prosecution's duty to disclose evidence applies to evidence to be used as part of their case-in-chief as well as rebuttal evidence (*People v. Hammond* (1994) 21 Cal. App. 4th 1611).

3. Bail

Bill Slocumb
1929 Truxtun Ave, Ste. C
Bakersfield, CA 93301
(661)324-1400

Attorney for Dave Douglass

IN THE SUPERIOR COURT OF THE STATE OF CALIFORNIA,
IN AND FOR THE COUNTY OF KERN

People of the State of California,	CASE NO. 123456
Plaintiffs,	NOTICE OF MOTION FOR OWN RECOGNIZANCE RELEASE OR IN THE ALTERNATIVE MOTION TO REDUCE BAIL
- v. -	
Dave Douglass,	
Defendant	DATE: October 16, 2017 TIME: 8:30 a.m. DEPT: CC
	Trial date: October 31, 2017 Readiness date: October 30, 2017

TO THE COURT AND THE DISTRICT ATTORNEY:

PLEASE TAKE NOTICE that at the date and time indicated above, or as soon thereafter as the matter can be heard in the above entitled court, the defendant will move for an order reducing the amount of bail set in this matter from _____ to an own recognizance release.

The motion will be made on the grounds that the bail set is excessive within the meaning of the Eighth Amendment to the United States Constitution and of Article I, §12 of the California Constitution.

The motion will be based on this notice of motion, on the attached declaration, the memorandum of points and authorities served and filed herewith, on all the papers and records on file in this action, and on such oral and documentary evidence as may be presented at the hearing of the motion.

Dated:

                        By   Bill Slocumb,
                        Attorney for Dave Douglass

DECLARATION IN SUPPORT OF BAIL MOTION

I, Bill Slocumb, Attorney for Defendant, declare:

Defendant is charged with Burglary with a gang enhancement. Defendant has no prior criminal convictions.

Defendant has extensive ties to the community.

Defendant is gainfully employed at _____. Defendant has been married for ____ years and has ____ children. Defendant's parents, brothers, and sisters also live in town as well as members of his extended family.

Defendant is, therefore, not a flight risk.

I so declare based on information and belief.

Dated:

                        By   Bill Slocumb,
                        Attorney for Dave Douglass

∞◊∞◊∞

Buzzy's Bail Bonds made a contribution to the production of this book which helps reduce the final cost to you, the consumer. They can be reached at (661)324-8119 to answer bail questions.

POINTS, AUTHORITIES, AND ARGUMENT

Article I, §12 of the California Constitution, which establishes a person's right to obtain release on bail from pretrial custody, prohibits the imposition of "excessive bail." The Eighth Amendment to the United States Constitution, applicable to California through the Fourteenth Amendment, prohibits the setting of a bail in an excessive amount.

Because bail was set per the county schedule, the amount was set without the court's attention to this individual defendant.

The United States Supreme Court has repudiated the concept of a disparate system of bail which requires those unable to post high bail (such as defendant, which under California law would require a premium of minimally 7% of total bail) to remain in custody while allowing the rich to obtain their freedom no matter how dangerous they may be. To the contrary, in *Stack v. Boyle* (1951) 342 U.S. 1, the court held that when bail is available, it must be fixed only in that the amount necessary to guarantee the bailee's appearance at trial. Any higher bail amount is excessive under the Eighth Amendment. California's Penal Code §1275 adds other factors to consider, as discussed below.

Since passage of Proposition 21 on the 1998 California ballot and subsequent legislative enactments, public safety has become the primary consideration in setting or denying bail. (*Penal Code §1275(a)*) Because the trial court may impose bail conditions intended to ensure public safety (such as directing Defendant to (a) wear an ankle monitor, (b) not travel outside the county, and (c) surrender his passport), reliance on an extraordinarily high bail such as was set herein is unwarranted.

While (1) public safety has been deemed the primary consideration in setting bail in the Court's discretion (*Griffin v. Superior Court* (1972) 26 Cal App 3rd 672, 702), in setting or reducing bail, the following factors must also be taken into consideration per California Constitution *Article I, § 12*; *Penal Code §1275*; (2) the seriousness of the offense charged; (3) the defendant's previous criminal record; and (4) the probability of the defendant appearing at hearing or trial of the case.

The charge in this case is serious, but the other factors weigh in favor of a bail reduction. (1) Defendant did not harm anyone and has not shown himself to be a danger to anyone, (3) Defendant's previous criminal record is non-existent, and (4) Defendant's ties to the community make the probability of him appearing for future hearings very high.

In *Van Atta v. Scott* (1980) 27 Cal. 3rd 424, 444, our Supreme Court ruled that the prosecution has burden of proof concerning a defendant's likelihood of appearing in court. The court stated, "Accordingly, it is concluded that due process requires the burden of proof concerning the detainee's likelihood of appearing for future court proceedings to be borne by the prosecution at the OR hearing".

In numerous cases our Supreme Court has declared expert predictions that persons will engage in future violent conduct to be unreliable and frequently erroneous (see *People v. Surnick* (1975) 14 Cal. 3rd 306, 326-327; *People v. Murtishaw* (1981) 29 Cal. 3rd 733, 767-775).

It is respectfully submitted that Defendant in this case is not a danger to society and that he will appear for all hearings as required.

∞◊∞◊∞

To help maximize your chances of obtaining an own recognizance release or a reduced bail, show the court as many ties to the community and as much support from family and friends as possible. Show the court that you have many reasons to stay in town and fight the charges against you and that it is unreasonable to believe that you would ever fail to appear.

It is good to show that you own a home, have a steady job, own a business in the area, or otherwise would suffer significant harm if you were to leave the area.

Get letters of support, such as one from your employer asking you to come back to work, one from your minister describing your religious activities, and even ones from your family explaining that you have an extended family with many supportive members that will stand by you and ensure that you go to court.

A typical bail motion asks the court to reduce bail without giving the court good reasons to grant the motion, but a typical bail motion is denied. Help your attorney show that you are not the typical defendant, and you should be given a reasonable bail because you are sure to appear for all of your hearings.

4. Lineup

Joe Whittington
1706 Chester Ave., Suite 304
Bakersfield, CA 93301
(661)322-5833

Attorney for Dave Douglass

IN THE SUPERIOR COURT OF THE STATE OF CALIFORNIA,

IN AND FOR THE COUNTY OF KERN

People of the State of California,	CASE NO. 123456
Plaintiffs,	MOTION FOR LINEUP BEFORE WITNESS
- v. -	FRED FRENCH
Dave Douglass,	DATE: October 16, 2017 TIME: 8:30 a.m.
Defendant	DEPT: CC
	Trial date: October 31, 2017 Readiness date: October 30, 2017

TO THE COURT, THE DISTRICT ATTORNEY, THE KERN COUNTY SHERIFF, AND COUNTY COUNSEL:

PLEASE TAKE NOTICE that at the date and time indicated above, or as soon thereafter as the matter can be heard in the above entitled court, the Defendant in this matter will move for an order directing the District Attorney of Kern County and the Kern County Sheriff to conduct a physical lineup in which the defendant will be exhibited to a witness in this case, Fred French.

This motion is made on the grounds that evidence of eyewitness identification is a material issue in this case and there exists a reasonable likelihood of mistaken identification, which a lineup would tend to resolve.

The motion will be based on this Notice of Motion, on the attached memorandum of points and authorities and filed herewith and such supplemental memorandum of points and authorities that may be hereafter filed with the court or stated orally at the hearing, on all of the papers and records on file in this action, or may be filed in this action, and on such oral and documentary evidence as may be presented at the time of the motion or related to this matter.

Dated:

By   Joe Whittington,
Attorney for Dave Douglass

DECLARATION IN SUPPORT OF MOTION

I, Joe Whittington, declare as follows:

1. I am the attorney representing the defendant in this action.
2. I have reviewed all of the police reports available to me and have interviewed the Defendant.
3. According to police reports, a man entered Mike's Market, approached cashier Fred French, and demanded money. Mr. French complied, and the man fled the scene.
4. Defendant was identified in a cross racial "face only" photographic lineup, but Defendant's physique is substantially different than the described suspect.
5. According to police reports, Mr. French described the man as a black male in his fifties, 6'0" to 6'1". When discussing the weight of the suspect, Mr. French indicated that the suspect weighed approximately the same as the interviewing officer, which was indicated by the officer to be 210 pounds.
6. However, according to booking reports, Defendant is 6'5" tall, weighs 250 pounds, and is 43 years old – Four or five inches taller, forty pounds heavier, and a decade younger.
7. Defendant's face may be similar to that of the suspect, but his physique, which has not been shown to witness Fred French, is substantially different.
8. Eyewitness identification is a material issue in this case because there is no substantial evidence to establish the Defendant as the perpetrator of the crime charged, other than eyewitness testimony.
9. There exists a reasonable likelihood of mistaken identification in this case because the eyewitness did not have a sufficient opportunity to observe the suspect, because of the nature of the offense charged and the allegation that a weapon was used. The eyewitness was subjected to pressures at the time of the incident that would affect his ability to

identify a suspect.
10. Your declarant believes that a lineup should be conducted while the incident is fresh in the mind of the eyewitness. At the preliminary hearing and at trial the defendant will be seated next to me at counsel table. Before the witness is subjected to a confrontation that is inherently suggestive or will reinforce a mistaken identification in his mind, a properly conducted physical lineup may remedy this danger.
11. Research has shown that there are certain lineup conditions which can increase the fairness and reliability of a lineup, such as exhibiting the subjects of the lineup in a sequential fashion, that is, displayed one at a time, rather than all at the same time. When compared to the traditional simultaneous lineup procedure, empirical studies show that sequential lineups produce a significantly lower rate of mistaken identifications.
12. Studies have shown that a witness looking at a simultaneous lineup is likely, despite any cautions, to want to pick someone. In so doing they are likely to pick the person who most closely resembles the actual perpetrator even if it is not the actual perpetrator.
13. This appears to be the error in the instant case in that the witness's description of the suspect significantly differs from physique of Defendant.
14. This tendency to select someone from the suspects presented is because the judgment that is made is a relative one. Sequential lineups, by contrast encourage witnesses to make absolute judgments, that is, compare a single face in a lineup to their memory, instead of deciding which of the several faces in the lineup most resembles the memory trace.
15. The defendant is currently in custody, confined at the Kern County Jail. It is submitted that the lineup should be conducted by the Sheriff's Department at the jail where there is a pool of possible participants which will enhance the possibility for a proper lineup.
16. It is further submitted that a total of ten persons should be in the lineup to prevent the witness from falling into the mindset that the suspect is one of six, as is often shown in popular television shows. This would consist of Defendant and nine others of similar appearance.

I declare that I am informed and believe that the foregoing is true and correct.

Dated:

By Joe Whittington,
Attorney for Dave Douglass

POINTS, AUTHORITIES, AND ARGUMENT

A DEFENDANT IS ENTITLED TO A PRETRIAL LINEUP IN AN APPROPRIATE CASE

In *Evans v. Superior Court* (1974) 11 Cal. 3rd 617, 623-625, the Supreme Court established the rule that in certain cases, a defendant may compel law enforcement agents to conduct a lineup.

> Because the People are in a position to compel a lineup and utilize what favorable evidence is derived therefrom, fairness requires that the accused be given a reciprocal right to discover and utilize contrary evidence. . . .
>
> We conclude in view of the foregoing that due process requires in an appropriate case that an accused, upon timely request therefor, be afforded a pretrial lineup in which witnesses to the alleged criminal conduct can participate. The right to a lineup arises, however, only when eyewitness identification is shown to be a material issue and there exists a reasonable likelihood of a mistaken identification which a lineup would tend to resolve.

A lineup's primary benefit arises before the witness encounters the defendant in court. Seeing a suspect among a group of individuals tests the accuracy of a witness's identification in a way different from an isolated encounter in the courtroom. For this reason, the value of a pretrial lineup may be diminished once a direct confrontation between defendant and accuser has occurred (*People v. Mena* (2012) 54 Cal. 4th 146, 154).

Because of the differences between Defendant and the description of the suspect, a lineup should eliminate Defendant as a suspect, but the Prosecution has declined Defendant's request for a lineup. Defendant, therefore, seeks an order from this Court requiring the Prosecution and the Sheriff to conduct a lineup.

COUNSEL HAS THE RIGHT TO BE PRESENT AT THE LINEUP

In *U.S. v. Wade* (1967) 388 U.S. 218 and *Gilbert v. California* (1967) 388 U.S. 263, the Supreme Court held that a pretrial lineup was a "critical stage" of the prosecution at which the accused was entitled to the presence of counsel. The court held that if a witness identified a defendant in a lineup conducted in violation of the defendant's right to counsel, subsequent in-court identifications by that witness were inadmissible unless shown by clear and convincing evidence to have an origin independent of the illegal lineup.

In *People v. Williams* (1971) 3 Cal. 3rd 853, 856, the Supreme Court described the role of counsel after the court orders a lineup pursuant to a motion by the defense.

> The above rules were adopted for two primary reasons: to enable an accused to detect any unfairness in his confrontation with the witness, and to insure that he will be aware of any suggestion by law enforcement officers, intentional or unintentional, at the time the witness makes his identification. It is not the moment of viewing alone, but rather the whole procedure by which a suspect is identified that counsel must be able to effectively reconstruct at trial. If defense counsel is to be able to intelligently cross-examine the witness, he cannot be excluded from the moment of identification any more than he can be excluded from the lineup itself. To hold otherwise would be to reduce counsel's cross-examination to little more than shooting in the dark, for he would not be fully apprised of what occurred at the, identification interview. For example, the defendant would have no way of knowing whether the witness was improperly led, whether the witness was hesitant or unsure in his identification, and he would not know what language or expressions the witness used. All of these factors could be very significant on cross-examination.
>
> (*Williams*, supra, internal punctuation and citations omitted)

A SEQUENTIAL DOUBLE BLIND LINEUP WILL ENHANCE THE POSSIBILITY OF A CORRECT IDENTIFICATION

Research has shown that there are certain lineup conditions which can increase the fairness and reliability of a lineup, such as exhibiting the subjects of the lineup in a sequential fashion, that is, displayed one at a time, rather than all at the same time. Further, the officers conducting the lineup should not know which suspect is associated with the matter under investigation (See, e.g. *United States v. Brown* (7th Cir. 2006) 471 F. 3rd 802, 804–05; *State v. Henderson* (2011) 208 N.J. 208, 248–49)

When compared to the traditional simultaneous lineup procedure, empirical studies show that sequential double-blind lineups produce a significantly lower rate of mistaken identifications.

Studies have shown that a witness looking at a simultaneous lineup is likely, despite any cautions, to want to pick someone. In so doing they are likely to pick the person who most closely resembles the actual perpetrator even if it is not the actual perpetrator. The judgment that is made is a relative one. Sequential lineups, by contrast encourage witnesses to make absolute judgments, that is, compare a single face in a lineup to their memory, instead of deciding which of the several faces in the lineup most resembles the memory trace. (See R.C.L. Lindsay & Gary L. Wells, *Improving Eyewitness Identification from Lineups: Simultaneous Versus Sequential Lineup Presentations* (1985) 70 J. Applied Psychology 556; Nancy Steblay, Jennifer Dysart, Solomon Fulero & R.C.L. Lindsay, *Eyewitness Accuracy Rates in Sequential and Simultaneous Lineup Presentations: A Meta–Analytic Comparison* (2001) 25 L. & Human Behavior 459; Jacqueline McMurtrie, *The Role of Social Sciences in Preventing Wrongful Convictions* (2005) 42 Am.Crim. L.Rev. 1271; Amy Klobuchar, Nancy K. Mehrkens Steblay & Hilary Lindell Caliguri, *Improving Eyewitness Identifications: Hennepin County's Blind Sequential Lineup Pilot Project* (2006) 4 Cardozo Pub.L. Policy & Ethics J. 381)

To further ensure accuracy, the witness should not be told how many persons he will be viewing; rather, he should be instructed:

> In a few moments, some individuals will be shown to you one at a time. Each person will be assigned a number and will be referred to only by number. Each will be asked to do certain things, such as turn. The person who committed the crime may or may not be included. While looking at the individuals, keep in mind that the individuals may not appear exactly as they did on the date of the crime. Their hairstyles, facial hair, clothing, etc., may have changed. The investigation will continue whether or not you make any identification. The officer conducting the lineup does not know which individual is a possible suspect. After each individual, the officer will ask you "Is this a person who robbed you?" Take your time answering the question. If you answer "yes", the officer will then ask you, "Can you describe in your own words how confident you are of the identification?" Even if you identify someone, the officer will continue to show you all of the individuals. Do you understand the procedure and other instructions I have given you?

5. Suppress

David Faulkner
422 Truxtun Ave
Bakersfield, CA 93301
(661)324-4777

Attorney for Dave Douglass

IN THE SUPERIOR COURT OF THE STATE OF CALIFORNIA,

IN AND FOR THE COUNTY OF KERN

People of the State of California,	CASE NO. 123456
Plaintiffs,	NOTICE OF MOTION AND MOTION TO SUPPRESS EVIDENCE
- v. -	
Dave Douglass,	DATE: October 16, 2017 TIME: 10:00 a.m.
Defendant	DEPT: CC
	Trial date: October 31, 2017 Readiness date: October 30, 2017

TO THE COURT AND THE DISTRICT ATTORNEY:

PLEASE TAKE NOTICE that at the date and time indicated above, or as soon thereafter as the matter can be heard in the above entitled court, the defendant will move the Court pursuant to the Fourth Amendment of the United States Constitution and *Penal Code §1538.5* for an order suppressing all evidence seized in the above entitled case including, but not limited to all officer observations, witness identifications, and all physical and intangible evidence seized or obtained as a result of search and seizure violations that occurred during the Defendant's detention, the search of Defendant's person, the search of Defendant's vehicle, the search of Defendant's abode, the search of Defendant's cell phone, the search of Defendant's computer equipment, and any other searches relevant to this case.

The motion will be based on this notice of motion, on the attached declaration, the memorandum of points and authorities served and filed herewith, on all the papers and records on file in this action, and on such oral and documentary evidence as may be presented at the hearing of the motion.

Dated:

                                             By   David Faulkner,
                                                      Attorney for Dave Douglass

DECLARATION IN SUPPORT OF MOTION TO SUPPRESS

I, David Faulkner, Attorney for Defendant, declare:

I am informed and believe that the search or searches complained of were without a warrant, or that any warrant was invalid, or that the fruits of any warrant were previously suppressed, or that there are other defects in the search or searches necessitating suppression in this matter.

Dated:

                                             By   David Faulkner,
                                                      Attorney for Dave Douglass

∞◊∞◊∞

> The court won't suppress evidence taken during a search just because the search was illegal. The defendant must also show standing. Standing is a showing that the defendant had a reasonable expectation of privacy in the place searched.

As examples, a person has a reasonable expectation of privacy in his own home, but he does not have a reasonable expectation of privacy in his neighbor's home. If the police conduct an illegal search of the neighbor's home while the defendant is present, the court will probably allow the illegally seized evidence to be used against the defendant, but not against the neighbor.

                    ~ David Faulkner
                      (661)324-4777

POINTS, AUTHORITIES, AND ARGUMENT

The fruits of an unlawful search must be suppressed (see *Fourth Amendment*, United States Constitution; *Badillo v. Superior Court* (1956) 46 Cal 2nd 269; *Alexander v. Superior Court* (1973) 9 Cal 3rd 387; *Penal Code § 1538.5*.)

The burden is on the Prosecution (*People v. Williams* (1999) 20 Cal 4th 119, 136).

The court in *Wilder v. Superior Court* set forth the proper procedure for a suppression motion when the seizure complained of was made without a warrant:

> The procedural problem arises from the fact that [the defendant], as the moving party, must necessarily file the first pleading-his motion to suppress evidence. Once [the defendant] has produced evidence to show that the seizure was without a warrant, [the prosecution] bears the burden of proving the only substantive issue at the hearing upon that motion-justification for the warrantless seizure. [citations]
>
> The obvious solution to this problem is a suppression motion pleading procedure whereby [the prosecution] speaks first to the issue upon which it bears the burden of proof and [the defendant] thereafter responds...
>
> ...if [the prosecution] fails to justify the seizure, [the defendant] wins his suppression motion whether or not [the defendant] asserts subsequent specific contentions.
> (*Wilder v. Superior Court* (1979) 92 Cal.App.3rd 90)

A warrant is required to search cellular telephone data (*Riley v. California*, 134 S.Ct. 2473) and stored communications (*18 U.S.C. 2701*, et. seq.)

6. Set Aside the Information

A Motion to Set Aside the Information is based only on the Information and the Preliminary Hearing transcript. The motion argues that the evidence presented at the preliminary hearing was not sufficient to support the Information. The motion cannot argue matters beyond the preliminary hearing. Even if the defendant has a perfect alibi, it cannot be argued in a Motion to Set Aside unless the evidence concerning the alibi was presented at the preliminary hearing. If the police reports show that defendant is completely innocent of the charged offense, the issue still cannot be raised in a Motion to Set Aside. A Motion to Set Aside is limited to matters found in the preliminary hearing.

The authority for the motion is found in *Penal Code §995*:

(a) Subject to subdivision (b) of Section 995a, the indictment or information shall be set aside by the court in which the defendant is arraigned, upon his or her motion, in either of the following cases:
  (1) If it is an indictment:
    (A) Where it is not found, endorsed, and presented as prescribed in this code.
    (B) That the defendant has been indicted without reasonable or probable cause.
  (2) If it is an information:
    (A) That before the filing thereof the defendant had not been legally committed by a magistrate.
    (B) That the defendant had been committed without reasonable or probable cause.

A Motion to Set Aside must refer to the transcript of the preliminary hearing. A common annotation used for this is RT, which stands for Reporter's Transcript. RT 4/19 refers to the Reporter's Transcript of the preliminary hearing, page 4 at line 19. RT 10-12 refers to pages 10 through 12 of the preliminary hearing transcript. The preliminary hearing transcript may also be referred to by other terms, such as TX. Thus, TX pg. 8, ln. 9, would refer to the Transcript of the preliminary hearing at page 8, line 9.

David Faulkner
422 Truxtun Ave
Bakersfield, CA 93301
(661)324-4777

Attorney for Douglass Duhan

IN THE SUPERIOR COURT OF THE STATE OF CALIFORNIA,
IN AND FOR THE COUNTY OF KERN

People of the State of California,	CASE NO. 123456
Plaintiffs,	MOTION TO SET ASIDE THE INFORMATION
- v. -	[*Penal Code §995*]
	DATE: October 16, 2017
Douglass Duhan,	TIME: 8:30 a.m.
	DEPT: CC
Defendant	Trial date: October 31, 2017
	Readiness date: October 30, 2017

TO THE COURT AND THE DISTRICT ATTORNEY:

PLEASE TAKE NOTICE that at the date and time indicated above, or as soon thereafter as the matter can be heard in the above entitled court, the defendant will move the Court under *Penal Code §995* to set aside the Information, alleging violations of:
1. Penal Code §459.5 – Shoplifting at Walgreens
2. Penal Code §459.5 – Shoplifting at Rite Aid
3. Penal Code §460(b)/664 – Attempted Burglary at Rite Aid
4. Penal Code §186.22 – Gang

The motion will be based on this Notice of Motion, on the attached memorandum of points and authorities and filed herewith and such supplemental memorandum of points and authorities that may be hereafter filed with the court or stated orally at the conclusion of the hearing, on all papers and records on file in this action and on such oral and documentary evidence as may be presented at the time of the motion.

Dated:

By David Faulkner,
Attorney for Douglass Duhan

POINTS, AUTHORITIES, AND ARGUMENT

Commitment without reasonable or probable cause within the meaning of *Penal Code §995* occurs if there is insufficient proof to establish a reasonable belief that an offense has been committed and the defendant is guilty of the offense charged. (*Caughlin v. Superior Court of San Diego County* (1971) 4 Cal 3rd 461; *People v. Hernandez* (1978) 90 Cal App 3rd 309).

"Probable cause is shown if a man of ordinary caution or prudence would be led to believe and conscientiously entertain a strong suspicion of the guilt of the accused." (*Bompensiero v. Superior Court of San Diego County* (1955) 44 Cal 2nd 178; see also *People v. Teale* (1965) 63 Cal 2nd 178; *People v. Shirley* (1978) 78 Cal App 3rd 424; and *Malleck v. Superior Court of San Francisco* (1956) 142 Cal App 2nd 396)

"Although the prosecution is not put to proof beyond a reasonable doubt in order to establish reasonable and probable cause before the magistrate, nevertheless the burden is on the prosecution to produce evidence that there is a reasonable probability, enough to induce a strong suspicion in the mind of a man of ordinary caution or prudence, that a crime has been committed and that defendant is guilty." (*Garabedian v. Superior Court* (1963) 59 Cal. 2nd 124)

There must be some evidence to support each and every element of an offense, or the finding must fall. (*Panos v. Superior Court* (1984) 156 Cal. App. 3rd 626; *People v. Superior Court (Mendella)* (1983) 33 Cal. 3rd 754; *People v. Shirley* (1978) 78 Cal. App. 3rd 424).

Count One Should be Dismissed

Jane Smith testified that she saw three men enter Walgreens (RT 21-23), make some noise down one of the isles, and then leave. After they left, Ms. Smith found packaging materials from electronics. Detective John Luke later identified Defendant from the surveillance videos (RT 128). Ms. Smith identified the person on the video as being the person who she saw earlier in the store (RT 133).

A pretrial identification procedure that is unnecessarily suggestive and conducive to mistaken identification constitutes a denial of due process. As stated by the United States Supreme Court in *Foster v. California* (1969) 394 U.S. 440, 442:

"[J]udged by the "totality of the circumstances," the conduct of identification procedures may be "so unnecessarily suggestive and conducive to irreparable mistaken identification" as to be a denial of due process of law."

A due process violation occurs when a pretrial identification procedure is so impermissibly suggestive that it gives rise to a very substantial likelihood of irreparable misidentification. (*People v. Blair* (1979) 25 Cal. 3rd 640, 659). The application of this rule depends on the circumstances of each case (*Simmons v. U.S.* (1968) 390 U.S. 377, 384-385), including whether the suggestiveness made the defendant "stand out" from the others in the lineup (*People v. Carpenter* (1997) 15 Cal. 4th 312, 367) and whether the identification procedure was unnecessary (*People v. Carter* (2005) 36 Cal. 4th 1114, 1162-1163, cert. denied, 547 U.S. 1099).

The defendant bears the burden of showing unfairness as a "demonstrable reality, not just speculation." The issue of constitutional reliability depends on whether the identification procedure was unduly suggestive and unnecessary (*Manson v. Brathwaite* (1977) 432 U.S. 98, 104-107). If the court determines such constitutional infirmity, the prosecution must demonstrate the identification itself was nevertheless reliable under the totality of the circumstances, taking into account such factors as the opportunity of the witness to view the suspect at the time of the crime, the witness's degree of attention, the accuracy of any prior description of the suspect, the level of certainty demonstrated at the confrontation, and the time between the crime and the confrontation. Without "clear and convincing" evidence of this reliability, the identification evidence is inadmissible. (*People v. Phan* (1993) 14 Cal. App. 4th 1453, 1461; *People v. DeSantis* (1992) 2 Cal. 4th 1198, 1222).

In the instant case, the identifications fail for two reasons. The first identification, by the officer, is without foundation and is improper expert testimony. The second identification, by the store worker, is also improper in that it is not an identification of the Defendant, but rather is simply the worker identifying the still photo from the video.

Even if there were sufficient evidence to indicate that Defendant committed an offense, that offense would be shoplifting, a misdemeanor, but there is insufficient evidence to indicate any felony offense. In passing Proposition 47, it was clearly the legislative intent that conduct, such as that alleged, should be charged as a misdemeanor.

Count Two Should be Dismissed

Mary Lamb testified that Kathryn Janeway reported that a subject entered Rite Aid. The subject placed items in a basket, later identified from video surveillance as being bottles of alcohol, and the suspect fled the store through an emergency exit (RT 72). Detective John Jones later viewed video recordings from Rite Aid and identified Defendant as the perpetrator (RT 138-139), and showed a lineup to Ms. Janeway, who identified the person on the video as being the person who she saw earlier in the store (RT 139).

The identification in this count fails for the same reasons discussed in Count One, the clerk did not identify Defendant, but rather only identified the person from the video as being the person who entered the store. The error in this identification process is obvious – no one has identified Defendant. One person simply identified the person shown in the video as the perpetrator, which may or may not have been Defendant.

Further, in this count as in Count One, even if there were sufficient evidence to indicate that Defendant committed an offense, that offense would be shoplifting, a misdemeanor, but there is insufficient evidence to indicate any felony offense. In passing Proposition 47, it was clearly the legislative intent that conduct, such as that alleged, should be charged as a misdemeanor.

Count Three Should be Dismissed

The prosecution did not produce evidence to indicate that any offense was committed as alleged in Count Three. The count should, therefore, be dismissed. Further, as with Counts One and Two, the offense level should be misdemeanor.

Count Four Should be Dismissed

Officer Bo Peep appeared as a gang expert and explained that the North Side Boys wear the color orange, have multiple subsets, and use hand signs to identify one another (RT 188). The officer theorized that several of Defendant's prior contacts with police indicate gang membership (RT 202). Officer Peep opined that if gang members committed a series of commercial burglaries (RT 230) that the burglaries would be for the benefit of the gang so that the merchandise (such as alcohol in the instant case) could be sold to purchase things such as guns for the purpose of committing murder (RT 233). The connection to the gang is "Obtaining items that can be sold for cash and obtaining cash" (RT 242).

Count Four alleges a violation *Penal Code §186.22(a)* (Criminal Street Gang). *Penal Code §186.22(a)* holds:

> Any person who actively participates in any criminal street gang with knowledge that its members engage in or have engaged in a pattern of criminal gang activity, and who willfully promotes, furthers, or assists in any felonious criminal conduct by members of that gang, shall be punished by imprisonment in a county jail for a period not to exceed one year, or by imprisonment in the state prison for 16 months, or two or three years.

There is insufficient evidence to believe that the conduct benefitted a gang or was anything other than for personal gain.

Based on the foregoing, Defendant respectfully requests that his motion be granted and the Information be set aside.

∞◊∞◊∞

A motion brought pursuant to *Penal Code §995* is based solely on the charging document (known as the Information) and the transcript of the preliminary hearing. Your attorney can't argue anything else.

Often, a defendant will know that the witnesses lied during the preliminary hearing, and he will have proof that they lied. A defendant may also have evidence establishing a strong alibi, or evidence proving that it was someone else who committed the crime, but none of these things can be brought up in a *Section 995* motion. Neither can a defendant show that the police reports, 911 calls, or witness statements contradict the preliminary hearing testimony. The defendant is restricted to the transcript of the preliminary hearing and is barred from pointing out evidence that would contradict it, no matter how obvious the evidence proving the defendant's innocence.

There will be a time to raise an alibi defense. There will be a time to show that the witnesses lied. There will be a time to implicate another person for the crime. That time is most often during trial, but the time is not during the hearing of a *Section 995* motion, unless the issues were raised during the preliminary hearing and are shown in the transcript of that hearing.

7. Recall Warrant

Larry Fields
2112 17th St
Bakersfield, CA 93301
(661)861-9750

Attorney for Danny Doggo

IN THE SUPERIOR COURT OF THE STATE OF CALIFORNIA,

IN AND FOR THE COUNTY OF KERN

People of the State of California,	CASE NO. 123456
Plaintiffs,	MOTION TO RECALL WARRANT
- v -	
Danny Doggo,	DATE: October 16, 2017 TIME: 8:30 a.m. DEPT: CC
Defendant	

TO THE COURT AND THE DISTRICT ATTORNEY:
    PLEASE TAKE NOTICE that at the date and time indicated above, or as soon thereafter as the matter can be heard in the above entitled court, the defendant will move the Court for an order to recall the warrant and set dates for further proceedings.

    This motion shall be based on this Notice of Motion, all papers and pleadings on file with the court and such oral and documentary evidence as may be presented at the hearing.

Dated:

                                      By   Larry Fields,
                                              Attorney for Danny Doggo

DECLARATION IN SUPPORT OF MOTION

I, Larry Fields, Attorney for Defendant, declare:

1. I am the attorney for Defendant in the above entitled matter.
2. The arraignment in this matter was set for June 30, 2017.
3. Due to a child care emergency, Defendant arrived after his case had been called, and the court issued a warrant.
4. I request that the warrant be recalled and that the matter be set for further proceedings.

I declare that I am informed and believe that the foregoing is true and correct.

Dated:

                                              _____
                                  By   Larry Fields,
                                         Attorney for Danny Doggo

POINTS AND AUTHORITIES

"Every court shall have the power to… provide for the orderly conduct of proceedings before it, or its officers." (*Code of Civil Procedure §128*)

∞◊∞◊∞

There is always a danger that the court will deny this motion and take the defendant into custody, but there is also the danger that the court will grant the motion and still take the defendant into custody because there is no valid bail bond on file.

To lessen this danger, talk to your bail bondsman before the hearing and ask if bail has been exonerated. If it has been, request that he file a resumption of bail.

8. Pitchess

Bill Slocumb
1929 Truxtun Ave, Ste. C
Bakersfield, CA 93301
(661)324-1400

Attorney for Douglass Duhan

IN THE SUPERIOR COURT OF THE STATE OF CALIFORNIA,
IN AND FOR THE COUNTY OF KERN

People of the State of California, Plaintiffs, - v. - Douglass Duhan, Defendant	CASE NO. 123456 MOTION FOR DISCOVERY OF PEACE OFFICER PERSONNEL RECORDS (*Pitchess*) DATE: October 16, 2017 TIME: 8:30 a.m. DEPT: CC Trial date: October 31, 2017 Readiness date: October 30, 2017

TO THE COURT AND THE DISTRICT ATTORNEY:

PLEASE TAKE NOTICE that at the date and time indicated above, or as soon thereafter as the matter can be heard in the above entitled court, the defendant will move the Court for an order permitting discovery and disclosure of the personnel records of the following peace officers pursuant to *Evidence Code §1043*, or alternatively an in camera review by the court of said documents and release of discoverable documents:
1. Deputy Dogg, Badge 1234
2. Deputy Danny, Badge 4567

The Agency or Agencies having custody and control of the records sought are:
1. The Kern County Sheriff's Department

The motion will be based on this Notice of Motion, on the attached memorandum of points and authorities, and filed herewith, and such supplemental memorandum of points and authorities that may be hereafter filed with the court or stated orally at the conclusion of the hearing, on all papers and records on file in this action and on such oral and documentary evidence as may be presented at the time of the motion.

Dated:

By Bill Slocumb,
Attorney for Douglass Duhan

SCHEDULE OF ITEMS SOUGHT

1. The records sought concern the above entitled case, now pending in this court.
2. The peace officers whose personnel records are being sought are those listed above.
3. The agency or agencies having possession of the records are listed above.
4. The type of records sought include documents relating to reports, complaints, and investigations of:
    a. Falsifying information;
    b. Illegal search and seizure;
    c. Excessive force;
    d. Omissions of information in reporting investigations;
    e. Dishonesty as the reporting of investigations; and
    f. Conduct unbecoming of a peace officer.

This request includes complaints of misconduct. The disclosed information should include names, addresses and phone numbers of people who have filed complaints against any of the named officers pursuant to *Evidence Code § 1045* (a) and *1043(b)*. (*Pitchess v. Superior Court* (1974) 11 Cal 3rd 531; *People v. Wheeler* (1992) 4 Cal 4th 284; California Constitution article I, section 28(d); *Chambers v. Superior Court* (2007) 42 Cal. 4th 673, 679; *Warrick v. Superior Court* (2005) 35 Cal. 4th 1011, 1019; *People v. Gaines* (2009) 46 Cal.4th 172, 179).

POINTS, AUTHORITIES, AND ARGUMENT

Law enforcement agency records maintained pursuant to *Penal Code §§832.5, 832.7* and *832.8(e)* are discoverable under *Evidence Code §1043* and *1045.*

> *Evidence Code §1045(a)* provides:
>
> Nothing in this article shall be construed to affect the right of access to records of complaints, or investigations of complaints, or discipline imposed as a result of such investigations, concerning an event or transaction in which the peace officer participated, or which he perceived, and pertaining to the manner in which he performed his duties, provided that such information is relevant to the subject matter involved in the pending litigation.

A defendant is entitled to discovery of information relating to an officer's personnel records where the accused shows the materiality of the subject matter of the pending case and a reasonable belief that that agency possesses the requested information. (*City of Santa Cruz v. Municipal Court* (1989) 49 Cal. 3rd 74, 84.) Evidence of a law enforcement officer's tendency to be dishonest in support of Defendant's theory in this case is relevant and admissible under *Evidence Code §1103.* (*People v. Memro* (1985) 38 Cal. 3rd 658; *Pitchess v. Superior Court* (1974) 11 Cal. 3rd 531, 537; *City of Santa Cruz v. Municipal Court* (1989) 49 Cal. 3rd 74, 84.) Likewise, evidence of an officer's excessive use of force/violence in the pending matter is relevant where the defendant is accused of resisting and delaying a peace officer.

Further, the only showing necessary is that the defense provide a plausible theory as how the discovery would be admissible for the court to grant the disclosure. (*Warwick v. Superior Court* (2005) 35 Cal. 4th 1011, 1026)

DECLARATION IN SUPPORT OF MOTION FOR DISCOVERY

I, Bill Slocumb, Attorney for Defendant, declare:

1. Defendant is presently charged with *Penal Code §243(b)* (Battery on a Peace Officer) and *Penal Code §148(a)(1)* (Resisting Arrest);
2. According to witness reports (attached), the named officers entered Defendant's residence without consent, handcuffed Defendant, then slammed him against a wall, forced him to the ground, and pepper sprayed him in the face.
3. Law enforcement reports (attached) differ from witness reports, but

confirm that physical violence was done to Defendant and that he was pepper sprayed.
4. I am informed and believe that during this investigation Defendant did not give consent for officers to enter his home as alleged in police reports. Defendant did not resist a lawful arrest as alleged in police reports. Officers used excessive force and violence against Defendant, and officers violated department policy when arresting Defendant.
5. The officer records are relevant and material because a substantial issue in the trial of this case may include dishonesty/truthfulness, illegal search and seizure, and not performing duties legally by the officers involved, as well as their credibility.
6. The materials requested are necessary for the proper preparation of this case for trial so as to locate and investigate witnesses to the character, habits, and customs of the peace officer involved to show that the peace officer acted in conformity with that character at the time of this incident and to impeach the testimony of the peace officer.
7. Declarant is informed and believes and alleges that said records are presently within the custody of the agency or agencies listed above, and Defendant has no other means to secure said information.

I declare that the foregoing is true and correct to the best of my knowledge and belief.

Dated:

By Bill Slocumb,
Attorney for Douglass Duhan

∞◊∞◊∞

If you've been arrested and are not a United States Citizen, remember that even the most minor charges can result in extreme immigration consequences.
~Andrew Fishkin, Immigration Attorney
www.lawyerfish.com
(661)322-6776

9. Withdraw Plea

Joe Whittington
1706 Chester Ave., Suite 304
Bakersfield, CA 93301
(661)322-5833

Attorney for Douglass Duhan

IN THE SUPERIOR COURT OF THE STATE OF CALIFORNIA,
IN AND FOR THE COUNTY OF KERN

People of the State of California,	CASE NO. 123456
Plaintiffs,	MOTION TO WITHDRAW PLEA
- v. -	
Douglass Duhan,	DATE: October 16, 2017 TIME: 10:00 a.m. DEPT: CC
Defendant	

TO THE COURT AND THE DISTRICT ATTORNEY:

PLEASE TAKE NOTICE that at the date and time indicated above, or as soon thereafter as the matter can be heard in the above entitled court, the defendant will move for an order to withdraw his no contest plea and enter a new and different plea. The motion will be made on the ground that Defendant's plea was not knowing and voluntary.

The motion will be based on this Notice of Motion, on the attached memorandum of points and authorities and filed herewith and such supplemental memorandum of points and authorities that may be hereafter filed with the court or stated orally at the conclusion of the hearing, on all papers and records on file in this action and on such oral and documentary evidence as may be presented at the time of the motion.

Dated:

                                          By   Joe Whittington,
                                                   Attorney for Douglass Duhan

POINTS, AUTHORITIES, AND ARGUMENT

Good cause to withdraw a plea is shown if the defendant did not exercise free judgment in entering into the plea. (*People v. Cruz* (1974) 12 Cal. 3rd 562, 566; *People v. Castaneda*, 37 Cal. App. 4th 1617; *People v. Huricks* (1995) 32 Cal. App. 4th 1201.)

Pleas may be set aside if defendants are unduly influenced to accept a plea because their counsel is obviously not prepared to proceed (*People v. Young* (1956) 138 Cal. App. 2nd 425), or the defendants represented by counsel entered into the plea as a result of fraud or duress. (*Penal Code §1018; Cruz*, supra, at 566; *Huricks*, supra; *People v. Dena* (1972) 25 Cal. App. 3rd 1001.)

In *People v. Stanworth*, 11 Cal. 3rd 588, the Supreme Court declared that defense counsel's ignorance of relevant, material facts or applicable law may constitute grounds for withdrawal of a plea. "Where the facts establish that counsel was ignorant of the facts or the law and it appears that such ignorance caused the withdrawal of a crucial defense, his client is entitled to relief."

DECLARATION IN SUPPORT OF MOTION TO WITHDRAW PLEA

I, Douglass Duhan, declare:
I am the defendant in this matter.
I entered a plea to serve a term of three years, but my plea was not knowing and voluntary based on the following facts:

1. My prior attorney told me that I was facing a maximum sentence of twelve years. It was only after I entered my plea that I learned I was actually only facing a sentence of six years.
2. I provided the appointed investigator with the name and phone number for my alibi witness, but no one contacted the witness. This left my prior attorney unprepared for trial and I felt that I had no choice other than to take a plea.
3. I was not informed of my right to compel the attendance of witnesses.
4. It was not until after I entered the plea that I learned my conviction would require me to register as a narcotics offender.
5. Had I known the above facts, I would not have entered the plea.

I declare that the foregoing is true and correct.
Dated:

By _____
Douglass Duhan, Defendant

10. Prohibit Restrictions on Right to Counsel

Elliot Magnus
641 H Street
Bakersfield, CA 93304
(661)395-0240

Attorney for Douglass Duhan

IN THE SUPERIOR COURT OF THE STATE OF CALIFORNIA,
IN AND FOR THE COUNTY OF KERN

People of the State of California,	CASE NO. 123456
Plaintiffs,	MOTION TO PROHIBIT RESTRICTIONS ON RIGHT TO COUNSEL
- v. -	
Douglass Duhan,	DATE: October 16, 2017 TIME: 8:30 a.m.
Defendant	DEPT: CC

TO THE COURT, THE KERN COUNTY SHERIFF, AND COUNTY COUNSEL:

PLEASE TAKE NOTICE that at the date and time indicated above, or as soon thereafter as the matter can be heard in the above entitled court, the defendant will move the court for an order directing the Sheriff of Kern County to remove the restrictions on the defendant's right to communicate confidentially with, and have access to, his counsel.

This motion will be made on the grounds that unless such private communications are guaranteed, the defendant will be deprived of the right to counsel under Article I, §15 of the California Constitution and the Sixth and Fourteenth Amendments to the United States Constitution.

This motion will be based on this notice of motion, on the attached declaration and memorandum of points and authorities served and filed herewith, on such supplemental memoranda of points and authorities as may hereafter be filed with the court or stated orally at the conclusion of the hearing on the motion, on all the papers and records on file in this action, and on such oral documentary evidence as may be presented at the hearing of the motion.

Dated:

By   Elliot Magnus,
Attorney for Douglass Duhan

SUMMARY OF RELIEF SOUGHT

By this motion, Defendant requests an order that Defendant shall be allowed unpaid, unmonitored telephone calls to his attorney and other persons designated by counsel to assist in the defense, which includes calls to the private investigator and paralegal assisting on this case.

POINTS AND AUTHORITIES

THE CONSTITUTIONAL RIGHT TO COUNSEL INCLUDES THE RIGHT TO COMMUNICATE BY TELEPHONE

The right of access to counsel is an essential component of the right of access to the courts. (*Bounds v. Smith* (1977) 430 U.S. 817).

This right is possessed not only by convicted prisoners, but by pretrial detainees who are jailed pending trial. (*U.S. ex rel. George v. Lane* (7th Cir. 1981) 718 F. 2nd 226, 230; *Lock v. Jenkins* (1981) 641 F. 2nd 488, 489.

Starting "from the premise that telephone communication is essential for inmate contact with attorneys," the court in *In re Grimes* (1989) 208 Cal. App. 3rd 1175 upheld a trial court order that the local jail must provide inmates a cost-free telephone line to the public defender's office. The court reasoned that the use of a collect-calls only system "unreasonably restricts communications between inmates at the jail and their attorneys."

Jail regulations restricting pretrial detainees' contact with their attorneys are unconstitutional where they "unjustifiably obstruct the availability of professional representation." (*Benjamin v. Fraser* (2nd Cir. 2001) 264 F. 3rd 175, 178).

"[P]rison administrators are in the best position to control inmates but this control cannot violate statutory or constitutional right (citation) Thus, the courts' traditional deference to administrative expertise in prison matters does not foreclose judicial intervention to remedy statutory or constitutional violations." (*In re Grimes* (1989) 208 Cal. App. 3rd 1175).

An inmate is entitled to "confidential consultation with attorneys" (*15 CCR §1068*). An in-custody defendant must be allowed "reasonable access to a telephone" (*15 CCR §1067*). Confidentiality rules apply not only to the attorney, but also to private investigators, paralegals, attorney employees, and other persons assisting in the defense (*15 CCR §3178*).

Jail procedures and regulations must be implemented so as not to invalidate a constitutional right. The standards set forth in Title 15 "constitute contemporary notions of decency and are advisory in nature," but the courts do not rely blindly on these standards as fixing constitutional minima. (*Inmates of the Riverside County Jail v. Clark* (1983) 144 Cal. App. 3rd 850, 860).

Defendant is allowed telephone calls now, so there is obviously no security or penological issue regarding defendant's use of the telephone. Defendant has been deemed to be indigent, and he receives the services of counsel at no cost to him.

Therefore, there appears to be no logical or legal reason to charge defendant for calls to the defense team or in having those calls monitored.

∞◊∞◊∞

Elliot Explains:

In my law practice, which is dedicated exclusively to the defense of criminal charges, I have used the types of motions presented in this book in almost every case I defend.

The motion above is especially important if a defendant has been denied confidential communications with his attorney. Effective representation requires effective communication, and those communications need to be confidential.

~Attorney Elliot Magnus (661)395-0240

11. Traverse

Larry Fields
2112 17th St
Bakersfield, CA 93301
(661)861-9750

Attorney for Dave Douglass

IN THE SUPERIOR COURT OF THE STATE OF CALIFORNIA,

IN AND FOR THE COUNTY OF KERN

People of the State of California,	CASE NO. 123456
Plaintiffs,	DEFENDANT'S MOTION TO TRAVERSE THE SEARCH WARRANT
- v. -	*(Penal Code §1538.5; Franks)*
Dave Douglass,	DATE: October 16, 2017
Defendant	TIME: 10:00 a.m.
	DEPT: CC
	Trial date: October 31, 2017
	Readiness date: October 30, 2017

TO THE COURT AND THE DISTRICT ATTORNEY:

PLEASE TAKE NOTICE that at the date and time indicated above, or as soon thereafter as the matter can be heard in the above entitled court, the defendant will move the Court for an order permitting cross-examination of the affiant in the affidavit filed in support of the search warrant issued and executed in this case and for a further order permitting the defendant herein to present evidence to controvert the factual allegations of this affidavit.

Thereafter, Defendant will move for an order suppressing all evidence seized in the above entitled case including, but not limited to, all officer observations, witness identifications, and all physical and intangible evidence seized or obtained as a result of search and seizure violations that occurred during any searches relevant to this case.

This motion will be made on the ground that the evidence seized pursuant to the warrant was the product of an unreasonable search and seizure in violation of the Fourth and Fourteenth Amendments to the United States Constitution and Article I, §13, of the California Constitution in that the affidavit in support of the above-mentioned warrant was defective by the omission of certain material facts and the inclusion of certain false statements described in the attached memorandum of points and authorities.

The motion will be based on this notice of motion, the attached declaration, the memorandum of points and authorities served and filed herewith, the records on file in this action and on such oral and documentary evidence as may be presented at the hearing.

Dated:

                              By   Larry Fields,
                                     Attorney for Dave Douglass

DECLARATION IN SUPPORT OF MOTION TO SUPPRESS

I, Larry Fields, Attorney for Defendant, declare:

I am informed and believe that the affiant omitted the following facts from affidavit in support of the search warrant in this matter and or inserted the following falsehoods:
1. The search of the residence was substantially complete prior to the issuance of the warrant.
2. The affidavit lists two probationers as living in the residence; however, each named probationer went into custody more than a month prior to the affidavit being signed.
3. The confidential informant noted in the affidavit is John Jones, who is the current husband of Defendant's ex-wife. This statement is made on information and belief.
4. Defendant was previously arrested by the affiant, but was cleared of all wrongdoing.

Dated:

                              By   Larry Fields,
                                     Attorney for Dave Douglass

POINTS, AUTHORITIES, AND ARGUMENT

A defendant may move to traverse a search warrant and to suppress the evidence seized based on that warrant on the ground that the search and seizure was unreasonable because there was not probable cause for issuance of the warrant. (See *Illinois v. Gates* (1983) 462 U.S. 213.

A warrant based on a false or misleading affidavit is invalid. The affiant in the instant case withheld information from the magistrate who issued the warrant and the affiant affirmatively misled the magistrate by inserting false statements.

The Supreme Court has held that a defendant may offer evidence at a suppression hearing to prove that some of the allegations in an affidavit supporting a facially sufficient search warrant were false. In order to obtain such a hearing the defendant must make a "substantial preliminary showing that a false statement knowingly and intentionally, or with reckless disregard for the truth, was included by the affiant in the warrant affidavit." (*Franks v. Delaware* (1978) 438 U.S. 154, 155)

Neither *Franks*, nor the cases following it, require an "intentional" false statement. Rather, the burden on the defense is merely to show an intentional or reckless disregard for the truth. (*People v. Panah* (2005) 35 Cal. 4th 395, 429). Evidence obtained pursuant to a search warrant based on an affidavit including false statements, or statements made in reckless disregard of the truth, must be suppressed. (*People v. Estrada* (2003) 105 Cal. App. 4th 783, 790; *People v. Thuss* (2003) 107 Cal. App. 4th 221, 224).

It is also clear that when an affiant incorporates information obtained from another law enforcement officer, the intentional/reckless standard also applies to that source of information. (*Franks v. Delaware* (1978) 438 U.S. 154, 163, fn. 6; *U.S. v. Roberts* (9th Cir. 1984) 747 F. 2nd 537, 546, fn. 10).

If the required preliminary showing is made, then the material that is the subject of the alleged falsity or reckless disregard is set to one side, and the affidavit's remaining content evaluated for probable cause. If there remains sufficient content in the warrant affidavit to support a finding of probable cause, no hearing is required, but if the remaining content is insufficient, the defendant is entitled under the Fourth and Fourteenth Amendments to a hearing.

The deliberate falsehood or reckless disregard must be that of the affiant, not of any nongovernmental informant. (*Franks v. Delaware* (1978) 438 U.S. 154, 171). However, if statements the affiant relied upon are demonstrated to be false and the affiant was unreasonable in believing the truth of such information, those facts must be excised from the affidavit and probable cause tested from the remaining truthful information. (*Theodor v. Superior Court* (1972) 8 Cal. 3rd 77, 100-101).

A defendant may attack a facially sufficient search warrant affidavit on grounds that, though it contains no affirmative falsehoods, it is incomplete. When an affidavit in support of a warrant contains omissions, the court must determine whether any of the asserted omissions are material. Omissions are "material" if they render the affidavit "substantially misleading." Material omissions can undermine the validity of a warrant when they are "made intentionally or with a reckless disregard for the accuracy of the affidavit." (*Franks v. Delaware* (1978) 438 U.S. 154, 171).

An omission which was recklessly inaccurate or was a deliberate attempt to mislead the magistrate, "undermines the judicial process, makes the entire affidavit suspect, and calls for harsh deterrence. The appropriate response is to quash the warrant regardless of whether the omission ultimately is deemed material." (*People v. Kurland* (1980) 28 Cal. 3rd 376, 391).

The entire point of the Fourth Amendment's search warrant requirement is that inferences be made and conclusions be drawn by the magistrate, not the officer seeking the warrant. Indeed, the failure of the officer to set forth the facts which form the basis for his opinion can be evidence of reckless conduct. (See *U.S. v. Alvarez* (5th Cir. 1997) 127 F. 3rd 372, 374, which noted that "While we decline to hold that the absence of [underlying] facts in the affidavit invariably converts negligence into recklessness for Fourth Amendment purposes, it is certainly one factor that must be considered in the analysis").

Once the material misrepresentations of fact are deleted and/or the material omissions of fact are added to the challenged affidavit, the probable cause analysis must follow the "totality of the circumstances test" (*Illinois v.* Gates (1983) 462 U.S. 213). Probable cause to issue a search warrant is found by looking at the "totality of the circumstances" contained within the four corners of the affidavit. (id. at 237). However, the court in *Gates* also warned that the magistrate must be provided with enough information to allow him to determine whether he is simply being provided with the "bare conclusions of others." (id. at 239).

In *United States v. Leon* (1984) 468 U.S. 897, 920, the Supreme Court held that evidence seized pursuant to an invalid search warrant would nevertheless be admissible "when an officer acting with objective good faith has obtained a search warrant from a judge or magistrate and acted within its scope." However, the "good-faith exception" does not apply if its application would allow the purpose of the exclusionary rule to be circumvented (i.e., deterrence of police misconduct.). Therefore, the exception does not apply when an affiant misleads the magistrate.

"Suppression therefore remains an appropriate remedy if the magistrate or judge in issuing a warrant was misled by information in an affidavit that the affiant knew was false or would have known was false except for his reckless disregard for the truth." (*Leon, supra* at 923).

∞◊∞◊∞

Tip from Tony:

You need an attorney. Every defendant does. The pleadings in this book are good to use as examples to help you understand the system, but they are no substitute for an attorney who has been educated and trained in the law. Neither this book, nor I, nor the best law professors are going to be able to make you an effective lawyer in time for your trial

I give my clients an aggressive defense. I fight for my clients, and sometimes the fight becomes so contentious that I have been charged with contempt. Contempt is a criminal charge, but I don't back down when my client's life or liberty is on the line; when I know I'm right.

Several years ago, I was charged with contempt. I was innocent. I do not deny that I am aggressive and, when appropriate, contentious and vehement in my manner, but I was not guilty. The fact that I knew I was innocent was not enough.

Even after graduating law school and practicing criminal defense for decades, I realized that I should not represent myself. It's just a bad idea. As a practical matter, a defendant cannot testify using the proper question and answer format. Further, if a defendant represents himself, each time he objects, the jury is likely to interpret it as the defendant trying to hide something. Self-representation in a criminal matter is simply a bad idea.

Effective representation requires an attorney. I used an aggressive attorney, like me, and he helped me win my case. You need an attorney also.

~J. Anthony Bryan,
Attorney at Law
(661)861-8050

12. Disclose Informant

Elliot Magnus
641 H Street
Bakersfield, CA 93304
(661)395-0240

Attorney for Doug Dave

IN THE SUPERIOR COURT OF THE STATE OF CALIFORNIA,

IN AND FOR THE COUNTY OF KERN

People of the State of California,	CASE NO. 123456
Plaintiffs,	DEFENDANT'S MOTION TO DISCOVER IDENTITY OF INFORMANT
- v. -	
Doug Dave,	DATE: October 16, 2017 TIME: 8:30 a.m.
Defendant	DEPT: CC
	Trial date: October 31, 2017 Readiness date: October 30, 2017

TO THE COURT AND THE DISTRICT ATTORNEY:

    PLEASE TAKE NOTICE that at the date and time indicated above, or as soon thereafter as the matter can be heard in the above entitled court, the defendant will move that the Court order the prosecution to disclose the true identity and present whereabouts of the informants in the above case, or dismiss the accusatory pleading.

    The motion will be made on the grounds that the informants are material witnesses on the issue of guilt or innocence in this action, and as such, the disclosure of the informants' identities are essential to a full and fair determination of the case.

    The motion will be based on this notice of motion, the attached declaration, the memorandum of points and authorities served and filed herewith, the records on file in this action and on such oral and documentary evidence as may be presented at the hearing.

Dated:

By Elliot Magnus,
Attorney for Doug Dave

DECLARATION IN SUPPORT OF MOTION TO DISCLOSE INFORMANT

I, Elliot Magnus, Attorney for Defendant, declare:

1. According to the affidavit in support of the search warrant in this case (attached), officers received information from a witness only identified as "X" that several people were involved in trafficking methamphetamine, including Defendant.
2. The officer begins by referring to X in the singular, but then changes to the plural form, thus indicating that X actually refers to more than one person: "X told me they know a white male subject… they told me they recently have seen [Defendant] in possession of a large amount of methamphetamine."
3. The affidavit goes on to explain that it is actually Bart Baddy who "holds the methamphetamine at his residence…"
4. These informants are alleged to have had knowledge as to who was in the home, who owned the home, and who was selling narcotics.
5. Defendant contends that another person was responsible for the drug sales (possibly one of the informants or Bart) and that Defendant had no connection with the narcotics.
6. A reasonable possibility exists that one or more of the informants, whose true number is unknown, was also an eyewitness to the crimes alleged and could give evidence on the issue of guilt or innocence in this action that would result in the exoneration of the Defendant.
7. Significantly, the informants each appear to know that "Bart" possessed the methamphetamine. This gives rise to an obvious third party culpability defense, and these informants can each give exculpatory testimony.
8. At a minimum, the informants should be able to testify that Bart owned the residence and possessed the methamphetamine that was found therein.
9. Further, the affiant makes conclusory statements concerning the reliability of the informants, but it is clear that X is representative of multiple people, some of whom may not be reliable and/or may have

themselves been involved in the sales of methamphetamine. The affidavit is unclear as to how many people are represented by X, why the officer believes one or more of them is reliable, and what portion of the information he received from each person represented by X.

Dated:

By Elliot Magnus,
Attorney for Doug Dave

∞◊∞◊∞

Why Every Defendant Needs a PI

We could discuss the many things a Private Investigator may do to uncover favorable evidence, but there are too many things to discuss on this one page or even in this one book.

It is easier to explain the advantages of having a PI with an example taken from a real case. Eddie was accused of chasing Kyle for more than a mile across uneven ground before knocking him down and shooting him with a gun. Four witnesses saw it. The police believed it to be an open and shut case.

The defense investigator walked the crime scene, reviewed the autopsy photos, talked to witnesses, looked at Eddie and Kyle's school yearbooks, talked to family members, reviewed old police reports, and did what he was supposed to do – he investigated.

The investigator learned that Kyle was a high school track star who was six inches taller than Eddie. Eddie had a bullet still lodged in his foot from an earlier incident, so he couldn't run. Each of the witnesses had reason to lie. One of the witnesses was also a high school track star, and he had a grudge against Kyle.

The defense investigator saved Eddie from a lifetime in prison by helping establish that Eddie was innocent.

Even if a defendant is not completely without guilt, a skilled private investigator can collect evidence to help a defendant get a better deal or have a better chance at trial. A licensed private investigator has the training and experience to know what types of evidence are most beneficial to a case and to know where to look to find that favorable evidence.

POINTS, AUTHORITIES, AND ARGUMENT

A DEFENDANT MAY MAKE A MOTION FOR AN ORDER REQUIRING THE PROSECUTION TO DISCLOSE THE IDENTITY OF AN INFORMER WHO IS A MATERIAL WITNESS ON THE ISSUE OF THE DEFENDANT'S GUILT

In *Honore v. Superior Court of Alameda County* (1969) 70 Cal. 2nd 162, 167, the California Supreme Court held that a motion for pretrial discovery is the proper vehicle for seeking disclosure of the identity of an informer who is a material witness on the issue of the guilt of the defendant.

> The record reveals that both in the municipal court and in the superior court defendants essentially sought only the disclosure of the identity of the informer because they deemed him to be a material witness on the issue of guilt. . . .The proper method of obtaining such information is by use of a motion for pretrial discovery and not by use of the procedure established by Pen C §1538.5.

THE DEFENDANT HAS MADE A PRIMA FACIE SHOWING OF MATERIALITY BY DEMONSTRATING THAT THERE IS A REASONABLE POSSIBILITY THE INFORMANTS MIGHT EXONERATE THE DEFENDANT

The California Supreme Court has established the burden of proof necessary to demonstrate a prima facie showing of materiality in order to require the disclosure of an informant's identity.

> [A] defendant seeking to discover the identity of an informant bears the burden of demonstrating that, "in view of the evidence, the informer would be a material witness on the issue of guilt and nondisclosure of his identity would deprive the defendant of a fair trial." (citations). That burden is discharged, however, when defendant demonstrates a reasonable possibility that the anonymous informant whose identity is sought could give evidence on the issue of guilt which might result in defendant's exoneration.
>
> (*People v. Garcia* (1967) 67 Cal. 2nd 830, 839-840).

To be a material witness, the informant need not be present at the time of the arrest. (*People v. Williams* (1958) 51 Cal. 2nd 355). A defendant need not demonstrate that an informant would give favorable testimony or show what the informant's testimony would be. (*People v. Tolliver* (1975) 53 Cal. App. 3rd 1036, 1043) Rather, the accused need only show that the informant was "in a position to perceive. . . either the commission or the antecedents of the alleged crime." (*People v. Ingram* (1978) 87 Cal. App. 3rd 832, 839) The controlling Supreme Court decisions have been analyzed as follows:

> . . .the evidentiary showing required by those decisions is not as to the exculpatory nature of the informer's potential testimony but merely as to the quality of the vantage point from which the informer viewed either the commission or the immediate antecedents of the alleged crime. The noted Supreme Court cases ask in effect, "What was the informer in a position to perceive?" If the evidence shows that the informer had a sufficiently proximate vantage point, those Supreme Court decisions simply speculate concerning the informer's potential testimony and hold that the defendant has demonstrated a reasonable possibility that the informant could give evidence which might result in the defendant's exoneration. Speculation as to such an informer's testimony is consistent with cases which discern a constitutional right in the accused to seek out the informer to inquire what he knows.
>
> *Williams v. Superior Court* (1974) 38 Cal. App. 3rd 412

THE COURT MUST ORDER THE PROSECUTION TO DISCLOSE THE IDENTITY OF AN INFORMER WHO WAS AN EYEWITNESS TO THE CRIME CHARGED AGAINST THE DEFENDANT

The identity of an informant who was an eyewitness to the crime charged against the defendant must be disclosed to the defense. In *People v. Goliday* (1973) 8 Cal. 3rd 771, 782, the Supreme Court held as follows:

> We emphasize that the eyewitness informers involved here acted as police agents at the time of the alleged sale. The police bear no duty to obtain information about a person who is not a material witness, who 'simply points the finger of suspicion toward a person who has violated the law.' [Citation omitted.] If, however, a material witness serves as an agent of the police and becomes a material witness on the issue of guilt, his desire for anonymity must yield to the interest of the accused in a fair trial. The police, accordingly, must undertake reasonable efforts to obtain information by which the defense may locate such an informer.

Likewise, in *People v. McShann* (1958) 50 Cal. 2nd 802, 808, the court stated:

> Disclosure is not limited to the informer who participates in the crime alleged. The information elicited from an informer may be 'relevant and helpful to the defense of the accused or essential to a fair determination of a cause' even though the informer was not a participant. For example, the testimony of an eyewitness-nonparticipant informer that would vindicate the innocence of the accused or lessen the risk of false testimony would obviously be relevant and helpful to the defense of the accused and essential to a fair determination of the cause.

Where the informant is an eyewitness to the transaction which is the basis for the charges against the defendant, the court cannot determine the materiality of the possible testimony of the informant without having the informant testify at an in-camera hearing (*People v. Ruiz* (1992) 9 Cal. App. 4th 1485).

THE COURT MUST ORDER THE PROSECUTION TO DISCLOSE THE IDENTITY OF AN INFORMER WHO IS A MATERIAL WITNESS ON THE ISSUE OF GUILT

The identity of an informant who is a material witness on the issue of guilt must be disclosed to the defense. This principle was articulated by the Supreme Court in *People v. Garcia* (1967) 67 Cal. 2nd 830, 838:

> In the instant case . . . we are concerned with informants who neither were participants in the alleged crime nor were eyewitnesses thereto. We have concluded that the relevant circumstances require that such informants be deemed material witnesses for the defense of defendant Garcia, and that the court's refusal to order disclosure of their identities upon proper request for such disclosure deprived defendant Garcia of a fair trial and requires that the judgment against him be reversed.

∞◊∞◊∞

> Like other human institutions, courts and juries are not perfect. One cannot have a system of criminal punishment without accepting the possibility that someone will be punished mistakenly.
> ~Antonin Scalia

13. Unseal Affidavit (Hitch Motion)

Bill Slocumb
1929 Truxtun Ave, Ste. C
Bakersfield, CA 93301
(661)324-1400

Attorney for Dean Dogg

IN THE SUPERIOR COURT OF THE STATE OF CALIFORNIA,
IN AND FOR THE COUNTY OF KERN

People of the State of California, Plaintiffs, - v. - Dean Dogg, Defendant	CASE NO. 123456 DEFENDANT'S MOTION TO UNSEAL THE AFFIDAVIT DATE: October 16, 2017 TIME: 10:00 a.m. DEPT: CC Trial date: October 31, 2017 Readiness date: October 30, 2017

TO THE COURT AND THE DISTRICT ATTORNEY:

PLEASE TAKE NOTICE that at the date and time indicated above, or as soon thereafter as the matter can be heard in the above entitled court, the defendant will move that the Court unseal the affidavit used to support the search warrant used in this case. An in camera hearing is requested pursuant to *People v. Hobbs* (1994) 7 Cal. 4th 948, to rule on the propriety of the concealing portions of the affidavit from the defendant.

This motion will be based on this notice of motion and memorandum of points and authorities served and filed herewith, on such supplemental memorandum of points and authorities as may hereafter be filed with the court or stated orally at the conclusion of the hearing on the motion, on all the papers and records on file in this action, and on such oral and documentary evidence as may be presented at the hearing of the motion.

Dated: _____

By Bill Slocumb,
    Attorney for Dean Dogg

DECLARATION IN SUPPORT OF MOTION TO UNSEAL THE AFFIDAVIT

I, Bill Slocumb, Attorney for Defendant, declare:

1. According to the affidavit in support of the search warrant in this case (attached), officers received information from a witness only identified as "X" that several people were involved in trafficking methamphetamine, including Defendant.
2. The officer begins by referring to X in the singular, but then changes to the plural form, thus indicating that X actually refers to more than one person: "X told me they know a white male subject… they told me they recently have seen [Defendant] in possession of a large amount of methamphetamine."
3. The affidavit goes on to explain that it is actually Bart Baddy who "holds the methamphetamine at his residence…"
4. These informants are alleged to have had knowledge as to who was in the home, who owned the home, and who was selling narcotics.
5. Defendant contends that another person was responsible for the drug sales (possibly one of the informants or Bart) and that Defendant had no connection with the narcotics.
6. A reasonable possibility exists that one or more of the informants, whose true number is unknown, was also an eyewitness to the crimes alleged and could give evidence on the issue of guilt or innocence in this action that would result in the exoneration of the Defendant.
7. Significantly, the informants each appear to know that "Bart" possessed the methamphetamine. This gives rise to an obvious third party culpability defense, and these informants can each give exculpatory testimony.
8. At a minimum, the informants should be able to testify that Bart owned the residence and possessed the methamphetamine that was found therein.
9. Further, the affiant makes conclusory statements concerning the reliability of the informants, but it is clear that X is representative of multiple people, some of whom may not be reliable and/or may have themselves been involved in the sales of methamphetamine. The affidavit is unclear as to how many people are represented by X, why the officer believes one or more of them is reliable, and what portion of the information he received from each person represented by X.
10. The affidavit contains an attachment, B, which has been sealed and withheld from Defendant. Attachment B may contain:
    a. Information related to Bart, his ownership of the house, and/or his possession of methamphetamine. This information would

be exculpatory as to Defendant.
   b. Information related to the reliability or lack thereof of informants represented by X. This too would be exculpatory to Defendant in that if the informants are reliable, their statements as to Bart owning the residence and possessing methamphetamine would tend to exonerate Defendant. If the informants are not reliable, the warrant was issued without probable cause.
   c. False statements of material facts or material omissions that could negate probable cause.
   d. Other information that is otherwise exculpatory and discovery is required under Brady.

Dated:

By Bill Slocumb,
    Attorney for Dave Douglass

POINTS, AUTHORITIES, AND ARGUMENT

WHERE AN AFFIDAVIT IN SUPPORT OF A WARRANT HAS BEEN SEALED, AN IN CAMERA HEARING MUST BE HELD BY THE COURT

In *Franks v. Delaware* (1978) 438 U.S. 154, 155-157, the United States Supreme Court held that a defendant may challenge the veracity of a facially valid warrant affidavit on a substantial preliminary showing that (1) the affiant made statements that were deliberately false or in reckless disregard of the truth; and (2) the affidavit's remaining content is insufficient to justify a finding of probable cause. The Fourth Amendment requires that a hearing be held at the defendant's request, where such a showing is made. The rule enunciated in *Franks* is, moreover, applicable to affidavits marred by omissions of fact (*U.S. v. Lefkowitz* (9th Cir 1980) 618 F. 2nd 1313, 1317).

However, our courts have recognized that when the defendant moves to traverse or quash a warrant on the grounds of material false statements or omissions in the application and the entire affidavit supporting it is sealed, the defendant may not be able to make even the minimal showing required by *People v. Luttenberger* (1990) 50 Cal. 3rd 1. Our Supreme Court has devised a procedure to address this issue. In this situation, the court is required to conduct an in camera hearing and failure to do so is reversible error (*People v. Galland* (2004) 116 Cal. App. 4th 489, 490-491).

No preliminary showing is required by the defendant to be entitled to an in camera hearing. By filing the motion, the court is required to treat the matter as if the defendant had made the requisite preliminary showing called for in *Luttenberger* (*People v. Hobbs* (1994) 7 Cal. 4th 948, 972).

THE COURT SHOULD FOLLOW A THREE PART PROCEDURE FOR THE IN CAMERA HEARING

In *People v. Hobbs* (1994) 7 Cal. 4th 948, 974-975 the court set forth the procedure for the in camera hearing. The prosecutor is present at the hearing and the defense excluded, unless the prosecutor consents to their presence. At the hearing the court should inform the prosecution what materials and witnesses it requires. The prosecution may present testimony. After examining the warrant and any supporting material or testimony, the court must determine the following:

> First, whether the affidavit is properly sealed, that is, whether sufficient grounds exist for maintaining the confidentiality of the informant's identity and whether a portion of the sealed information may be disclosed without compromising the informant's identity.

> Second, if the court finds that the affidavit, or a major part of it, has been properly sealed, the court proceeds to the next step, which requires the court to determine whether "there is a reasonable probability the defendant would prevail" on his suppression motion. The "precise standard of review" applied by the court at this stage of the *Hobbs* procedure depends on whether the defendant has noticed a motion to quash the warrant or to traverse it.

> Third, if the affidavit is found to be properly sealed and the defendant has filed a motion to traverse, the court must determine whether the defendant's allegations of material misrepresentations or omissions are supported by the record under the standards set out in *Franks v. Delaware* (1978) 438 U.S. 154, 155-156, which is that the affidavit supporting the search warrant contained inaccurate statements or omissions from the affidavit that rendered it substantially misleading, meaning that there was a substantial possibility that the misrepresentations would have altered a reasonable magistrate's probable cause determination.

The instant motion goes to the first step, with the expectation that a motion to traverse (steps two and three) may be brought based on the contents of the sealed affidavit, if such is disclosed.

Since the defendant is completely ignorant of all critical portions of the affidavit (and, as a result, the defense is unable to specify what materials the court should reveal in camera), the court must take it upon itself both to examine the affidavit for possible inconsistencies or insufficiencies regarding the showing of probable cause, and inform the prosecution of the materials or witnesses it requires. The materials will invariably include such items as relevant police reports and other information regarding the informant and the informant's reliability (*People v. Hobbs* (1994) 7 Cal. 4th 948, 973).

Furthermore because defendant's access to the "essence of the affidavit" has been eliminated, the court may, in its discretion, find it necessary and appropriate to call and question the affiant, the informant, or any other witness whose testimony it deems necessary to rule upon the issues. Where feasible, the court may also, in its discretion, order the tape recording or videotaping of all or any portion of the in camera proceeding (*People v. Hobbs* (1994) 7 Cal. 4th 948).

∞◊∞◊∞

Slocumb Says:

I have tried over 100 cases to jury verdict, including murder, kidnapping, robbery, child molestation, domestic violence, drug and alcohol cases, but I have resolved many more cases by use of motions, such as the one above. Only a small percentage of cases go all the way to trial. Most cases are resolved with a motion or a plea, but a lot of preparation is required before a case is ready to be resolved. Investigation and legal research are almost always required, but sometimes effective preparation also requires testing and examination by experts.

When I was a prosecutor, I handled matters from filing through trial, so I understand both sides of a case. I know a case's strengths and weaknesses, and I understand when experts can help. I have working relationships with experts and investigators who all contribute a successful defense of a case. The value of these experts should not be underestimated.

~ Bill Slocumb, Attorney at Law
(661)324-1400

14. Enforce Agreement

Joe Whittington
1706 Chester Ave., Suite 304
Bakersfield, CA 93301
(661)322-5833
Attorney for Dave Douglass

IN THE SUPERIOR COURT OF THE STATE OF CALIFORNIA,
IN AND FOR THE COUNTY OF KERN

People of the State of California,	CASE NO. 123456
Plaintiffs,	DEFENDANT'S MOTION TO ENFORCE AGREEMENT
- v. -	DATE: October 16, 2017
Dave Douglass,	TIME: 10:00 a.m.
	DEPT: CC
Defendant	Trial date: October 31, 2017
	Readiness date: October 30, 2017

TO THE COURT AND THE DISTRICT ATTORNEY:

PLEASE TAKE NOTICE that on the date and time indicated above, or as soon thereafter as the matter may be heard in the above-entitled Court, the Defendant will move to dismiss the accusatory pleading.

The motion will be made on the grounds that the prosecution is barred by Double Jeopardy in that Defendant already entered into a plea bargain and Defendant is entitled to the benefit of the bargain.

The motion will be based on this notice of motion, on the memorandum of points and authorities served and filed herewith, on the records on file in this action, and on such oral and documentary evidence as may be presented at the hearing on the motion.

Dated:

By Joe Whittington,
Attorney for Dave Douglass

POINTS, AUTHORITIES, AND ARGUMENT

STATEMENT OF THE CASE

Multiple cases were pending against Defendant:

- Case 987654, alleging Possession for Sale (*Health and Safety §11378*) stemming from a June 31, 2017 was dismissed for insufficient cause.
- Cases 765432 and 345678 were dismissed in the interest of justice.
- Case 234567 was resolved by a plea bargain in which Defendant pled to *Health and Safety §11379(a)* in exchange for a five year sentence
- Case 456789 was resolved by a plea bargain in which Defendant pled to *Vehicle Code §10851(a)* in exchange for a three year concurrent sentence

The instant case, 123456, Defendant is charged with Possession for Sale (*Health and Safety §11378*) stemming from a June 31, 2017 search of his home – the exact allegations of dismissed case 987654. The plea bargain was meant to encompass and resolve all allegations against Defendant, but the Prosecution violated the agreement by filing the instant case the day after the plea bargain was made.

THE PROSECUTION IS BARRED BY DOUBLE JEOPARDY

The double jeopardy clause of Fifth Amendment guarantees that no person shall be subject for the same offense to be twice put in jeopardy of life or limb, and it is made applicable to the states through the due process clause. Protection against double jeopardy is also embodied in California Constitution Article I §15. The California Constitution is a document of independent force and effect that may be interpreted in a manner more protective of a defendant's rights than the Federal Constitution.

In California, a court's inquiry is thus guided by the decisions announcing the minimum standards of double jeopardy protection under the Fifth Amendment, as well as the decisions interpreting the California Constitution and the statutory provisions implementing those constitutional protections. (*People v. Fields* (1996) 13 Cal. 4th 289, 297-298; see also *Penal Code §1023*).

Defendant's plea bargain encompassed and resolved all known matters concerning him. Defendant has already been in jeopardy from matters stemming from the June 31, 2017 search of his home.

THE PROSECUTION IS BOUND TO THE TERMS OF ITS CONTRACTS

Courts interpret plea agreements according to contract principles, (*Santobello v. New York* (1971) 404 U.S. 257, 262-63), and the agreements should be enforced using the same principles (*United States v. Schuman* (9th Cir 1997) 127 F. 3rd 815, 817; *People v. Bobbit* (2006) 138 Cal. App. 4th 445; People v. Shelton (2006) 37 Cal. 4th 759).

Just as with other forms of contracts, a negotiated guilty plea is a "bargained for quid pro quo." (*United States v. Escamilla* (9th Cir 1992) 975 F. 2nd 568, 571; *People v. Gipson* (2004) 117 Cal. App. 4th 1065). When a defendant performs his side of the bargain, the Prosecution is also required to perform its duty. A defendant is entitled to the benefit of the bargain. (*United States v. Hyde* (1997) 520 U.S. 670).

THE DEFENDANT IS ENTITLED TO COMPEL THE SPECIFIC PERFORMANCE OF A PLEA AGREEMENT

The Supreme Court, in *Santobello v. New York* (1971) 404 U.S. 257, explained the right to enforce a plea bargain in the following manner:

> This phase of the process of criminal justice, and the adjudicative element inherent in accepting a plea of guilty, must be attended by safeguards to insure the defendant what is reasonably due in the circumstances. Those circumstances will vary, but a constant factor is that when a plea rests in any significant degree on a promise or agreement of the prosecutor, so that it can be said to be part of the inducement or consideration, such promise must be fulfilled.

When a defendant has detrimentally relied on promises made by the prosecution, such as in the instant case, he or she may obtain specific performance of those promises. (See for example *Santobello v. New York* (1971) 404 U.S. 257; *United States v. McCray* (8th Cir 1988) 849 F. 2nd 304, 306; *In re Kenneth H.* (2000), 80 Cal. App. 4th 143; *People v. Mancheno* (1982) 32 Cal. 3rd 855; *People v. Thornton* (2006) 137 Cal. App. 4th 241; *People v. Rhoden* (1999) 75 Cal. App. 4th 1346, 1355).

Defendant bargained for resolution of all pending matters in exchange for a lengthy prison sentence. The Prosecution should be bound to the agreement and the instant case should be dismissed.

15. Sanctions (Trombetta Motion)

David Faulkner
422 Truxtun Ave
Bakersfield, CA 93301
(661)324-4777
Attorney for Dave Douglass

IN THE SUPERIOR COURT OF THE STATE OF CALIFORNIA,
IN AND FOR THE COUNTY OF KERN

People of the State of California,	CASE NO. 123456
Plaintiffs,	DEFENDANT'S MOTION TO DISMISS FOR LOSS OF EVIDENCE
- v. -	[*Trombetta*]
Dave Douglass,	DATE: October 16, 2017
Defendant	TIME: 8:30 a.m.
	DEPT: CC
	Trial date: October 31, 2017
	Readiness date: October 30, 2017

TO THE COURT AND THE DISTRICT ATTORNEY:

PLEASE TAKE NOTICE that at the date and time indicated above, or as soon thereafter as the matter can be heard in the above entitled court, Defendant will move for an order dismissing the above entitled action because of the loss of significant exculpatory evidence.

This motion will be based upon this notice of motion, the memorandum of points and authorities served and filed concurrently herewith, on all the papers and records on file in this action, and on such oral and documentary evidence as may be presented at the hearing of this motion.

Dated:

_____
By David Faulkner,
Attorney for Dave Douglass

STATEMENT OF THE CASE

Kyle Knight reported that he saw a male and a female tampering with his neighbor's vehicle (RT 5) and attempting to open the doors. However, he did not specify who was doing what to the vehicle (RT 16). His report led officers to stop Defendant and her codefendant's vehicle, and Mr. Knight identified them as the suspects (RT 6). The vehicle's owner, Valentine Victim, reported that the vehicle's tow hitch was missing and a strap was burnt (RT 7-8), but he gave no indication of when he last observed those portions of the vehicle.

The vehicle was locked and had an alarm active (RT 7), but no one reported that the alarm went off. No tow hitch was found on either defendant or in their vehicle (RT 12), and law enforcement did not seize any tools capable of removing a tow hitch (id.). Nor did law enforcement seize or even document any items that could reach a temperature high enough to burn the vehicle's straps. Fingerprints were taken from the vehicle handles, but the fingerprints were not a match to either defendant (RT 10).

MEMORANDUM OF POINTS AND AUTHORITIES

THE PROSECUTION HAD A DUTY IN THIS CASE TO PRESERVE THE VICTIM'S VEHICLE AND THE CODEFENDANT'S VEHICLE

The law does not impose a duty on the prosecution to collect evidence that might be beneficial to the defense; however, once collected, the prosecution does have a duty to preserve material evidence. (*In re Michael L.* (1985) 39 Cal 3rd 81; *People v. Hogan* (1982) 31 Cal 3rd 815, 851, disapproved on other grounds in *People v. Cooper* (1991) 53 Cal 3rd 771, 836).

In this case, law enforcement seized control of the victim's vehicle and co-defendant's vehicle along with the tools and other evidence therein, but failed to preserve the vehicles or evidence for use by Defendant. The prosecution further failed to even photograph or inventory items in either vehicle.

THE LOST EVIDENCE WAS MATERIAL TO THE DEFENSE CASE

If the prosecution preserved and then destroyed or permanently lost evidence, the defense may make a motion for sanctions, called a *Trombetta* or *Youngblood* motion. The destroyed evidence must have been material to the defense case (*California v. Trombetta* (1984) 467 US 479, 488).

The materiality of evidence in California is determined under the *Trombetta/Youngblood* federal standard (*People v. Zapien* (1993) 4 Cal 4th 929, 964; *People v. Cooper* (1991) 53 Cal 3rd 771, 810; People v. Johnson (1989) 47 Cal 3rd 1194, 1233). Material evidence is evidence that might be expected to play a significant role in the suspect's defense. It must possess an exculpatory value that was apparent before the evidence was lost or destroyed, and be of such a nature that the defendant would be unable to obtain comparable evidence by other reasonably available means. (*California v. Trombetta*, supra.)

The lost vehicles are material to Defendant's case because the codefendant's vehicle could be used to show not only that Defendant did not have the means to commit the charged offense, but also that if any offense was actually committed, it was not by her or her codefendant. Simply put, the loss and the required means to commit the offense were not in the codefendant's vehicle, and there was simply no other reasonable place the items could be found. Further, the victim's vehicle could be used to show that Defendant had no contact at all with the vehicle. If Defendant did have contact with the vehicle, her DNA would have necessarily been transferred to the vehicle.

Law enforcement's release of the vehicles has summarily denied Defendant the right to present favorable and material evidence that would play a significant role in his defense. The investigative officers are now at liberty to give their own inculpatory description of the vehicles and their contents, which could have been contradicted by the access to the vehicles in several ways.

First, had the defense been granted access to the codefendant's vehicle before its release – the vehicle in which she was arrested, the vehicle could be thoroughly examined to establish that the "stolen" hitch was not in the vehicle. Because defendant was stopped shortly after the offense, the absence of the hitch is exculpatory. Without access to the vehicle, the prosecution is free to impeach law enforcement's investigation and argue that the arresting officers simply did not conduct a thorough enough search to find the hitch that was carefully hidden by defendants. A skilled prosecutor could simply ask questions like, "did you search inside the glove box?", "did you search the trunk?", "did you search under the hood?" Any negative answer could be used to argue that defendants could have hidden the hitch beyond the scope of law enforcement's search.

Second, had the defense been granted access to the vehicle before its release, the defense could have shown that none of the "tools" allegedly found in the vehicle could have been used to remove the hitch. Without access to the tools, the Prosecution is free to argue that the defendants had "burglary tools" that could have been used to remove the hitch.

Third, had the defense been granted access to the vehicle before its release, the defense could have shown that defendant's had no ability to cause the burn damage to the victim's vehicle. Without access to the vehicle, the Prosecution is free to argue that the defendants had torches or some other ignition source hidden in the vehicle.

Fourth, had the defense been granted access to the victim's vehicle before its release, the defense could have shown that the vehicle alarm would have gone off if the vehicle was manipulated as described by the witness. This is significant exculpatory evidence that could have disproved the witness's description of events.

Finally, had the defense been granted access to the victim's vehicle before its release, the defense could have shown that the "straps" on the gas can, made of metal on many vehicle models, could not be burnt except by high temperature such as would have ignited the gas cans.

The loss of the victim's vehicle is also damning to Defendant. Had the vehicle been preserved, DNA testing could have eliminated Defendant as a suspect in that his DNA would not have been found on the door handles, the area around the receiver hitch, or anywhere else on the vehicle.

THE APPROPRIATE SANCTION IN THIS CASE IS DISMISSAL

This Court should dismiss the instant action because Defendant is irreparably harmed by the loss of the described evidence.

16. Dismiss for Speedy Trial Violation

Joe Whittington
1706 Chester Ave., Suite 304
Bakersfield, CA 93301
(661)322-5833

Attorney for Dave Daniels

IN THE SUPERIOR COURT OF THE STATE OF CALIFORNIA,

IN AND FOR THE COUNTY OF KERN

People of the State of California,	CASE NO. 123456
Plaintiffs,	DEFENDANT DAVE DANIELS'S MOTION TO DISMISS
- v. -	(Penal Code §1382(2); Speedy Trial)
Dave Daniels,	DATE: October 16, 2017
Defendant	TIME: 10:00 a.m.
	DEPT: CC
	Trial date: October 31, 2017
	Readiness date: October 30, 2017

TO THE COURT AND THE DISTRICT ATTORNEY:
    PLEASE TAKE NOTICE that at the date and time indicated above, or as soon thereafter as the matter can be heard in the above entitled court, the defendant will move for an order dismissing the action.

    The motion will be made on the grounds that the defendant was denied the statutory right to a speedy trial as guaranteed by *Penal Code §1382(2)* because the defendant was not brought to trial within 60 days after the filing of the information and there was no good cause for the delay beyond this period of time.

    The motion will be based on this notice of motion, the attached declaration, the memorandum of points and authorities served and filed herewith, the records on file in this action and on such oral and documentary evidence as may be presented at the hearing.

Dated:

By Joe Whittington,
    Attorney for Dave Daniels

POINTS, AUTHORITY, AND ARGUMENT

When there has been a statutory violation of a defendant's right to a speedy trial, the prosecution must show good cause or the matter must be dismissed.

Penal Code §1382(a)(2) provides in part:

> The court, unless good cause to the contrary is shown, shall order the action to be dismissed in the following cases: . . .
> (2) When a defendant is not brought to trial in a superior court within 60 days after the finding of the indictment or filing of the information....

In *Overby v. Municipal Court* (1981) 121 Cal. App. 3rd 377, 382, the court held that a violation of this statutory right to speedy trial results in dismissal of the action, unless good cause for the continuance can be established:

> When there has been a violation of the statutory guarantee of a speedy trial constitutional right, prejudice to the accused is presumed. He need not make any showing of actual prejudice. There is no balancing of his prejudice against the People's justification. Rather, the People have the burden of showing good cause for delay.

Court congestion does not constitute good cause for delay under the requirements of *Penal Code §1382*. (*Rhinehart v. Municipal Court* (1984) 35 Cal. 3rd 772, 781 (1984); *People v. Johnson* (1980) 26 Cal. 3rd 557)

A defendant must be "brought to trial" within the statutory period or the case must be dismissed unless good cause is shown. The court in *Rhinehart v. Municipal Court* (1984) 35 Cal. 3rd 772, 780, ruled that:

> an accused is 'brought to trial' within the meaning of section 1382 when a case has been called for trial by a judge who is normally

available and ready to try the case to conclusion. The court must have committed its resources to the trial, and the parties must be ready to proceed and a panel of prospective jurors must be summoned and sworn.

In the instant case, Defendant was not brought to trial within the statutory period and the Prosecution has not shown good cause for the delay.

∞◊∞◊∞

Whittington's Wisdom:

The motion above is just one type of motion to dismiss I use, but a motion to dismiss is not practical in every case. In addition to motions to dismiss discussed in this book (Set *Aside the Information, Sanctions, Dismiss for Speedy Trial Violation,* and *Dismiss for Delay in Prosecution*), I bring other types of motions to dismiss, including:

- *Suggestion to Dismiss (Penal Code §1385)* – This catchall dismissal motion can be brought when logic indicates a case should be dismissed, such as dismissal of a minor theft case so a defendant can enter the military.

- *Dismiss for Selective Prosecution* – If it can be shown that a defendant is being prosecuted because of his race, sexual orientation, religion or for some other improper reason, a motion to dismiss may be brought as discussed in *Murgia v. Municipal Court* (1975) 15 Cal. 3rd 286.

- *Motion to Dismiss Under Penal Code §1387* – If a case has been dismissed for lack of probable cause, speedy trial violations, or for other reasons, but the prosecution refiles the case. A *Motion to Dismiss Under Penal Code §1387* can at times put a final end to a case based on technical rules.

- *Motion to Dismiss for Interrupted Preliminary Hearing* – Penal Code *§861* gives a felony defendant the right to an uninterrupted preliminary hearing. If some of the prosecution witnesses don't show up or leave so that the hearing is not finished in one session, the case may be dismissed.

Effective representation requires creativity, hard work, and an arsenal of motions, including multiple types of motions to dismiss.

~Joe Whittington, Attorney at Law
(661)322-5833

17. Dismiss for Delay in Prosecution

Larry Fields
2112 17th St
Bakersfield, CA 93301
(661)861-9750
Attorney for Dave Douglass

IN THE SUPERIOR COURT OF THE STATE OF CALIFORNIA,
IN AND FOR THE COUNTY OF KERN

People of the State of California,	CASE NO. 123456
Plaintiffs,	DEFENDANT'S MOTION TO DISMISS FOR DELAY IN PROSECUTION
- v. -	
Dave Douglass,	DATE: October 16, 2017 TIME: 10:00 a.m.
Defendant	DEPT: CC
	Trial date: October 31, 2017 Readiness date: October 30, 2017

TO THE COURT AND THE DISTRICT ATTORNEY:

PLEASE TAKE NOTICE that on the date and time noted above or as soon thereafter as counsel may be heard in the courtroom of the above-entitled court, the defendant will move for an order to Dismiss for Delay in Prosecution.

This motion is made on the ground that the Prosecution team intentionally and/or unreasonably delayed proceedings and Defendant was prejudiced by the delay.

The motion will be based on this Notice of Motion, on the attached memorandum of points and authorities and filed herewith and such supplemental memorandum of points and authorities that may be hereafter filed with the court or stated orally at the conclusion of the hearing, on all papers and records on file in this action and on such oral and documentary evidence as may be presented at the time of the motion.
Date:

By Larry Fields,
    Attorney for Dave Douglass

POINTS, AUTHORITY, AND ARGUMENT

STATEMENT OF THE CASE

The following summary is based on the available records, including reports provided in discovery and the Court's files.

On or about April 5, 2008, Defendant was arrested and released without an appearance date being set. The citation issued contains a signature line following the statement, "Without admitting guilt, I promise to appear at the time and place indicated below." On the signature line is simply printed, "In Custody" and no date or time is given.

A Complaint was not filed until April 29, 2008, and Defendant was not notified of the Complaint until he was re-arrested on August 5, 2015.

During the delay of more than seven years, Defendant lived an open and public life. He reported his correct address on his tax forms, employment forms, and other records that were readily available to law enforcement. Law enforcement could have easily located and arrested Defendant, but they chose not to do so until more than seven years after the Complaint was filed.

MEMORANDUM OF POINTS AND AUTHORITIES

A DEFENDANT'S CONSTITUTIONAL RIGHT TO A SPEEDY TRIAL ATTACHES AFTER THE FILING OF A COMPLAINT

The Sixth Amendment to the United States Constitution provides in part: "In all criminal prosecutions, the accused shall enjoy the right to a speedy and public trial. . . ." Article I, section 13, of the California Constitution states that: "In criminal prosecutions, in any court whatever, the party accused shall have the right to a speedy and public trial. . . ." (See also *Penal Code §686*).

Our Supreme Court has held that, "[t]he right to a speedy trial is a fundamental right granted to the accused and . . . the policy of the law since the time of the promulgation of Magna Charta and the Habeas Corpus Act. . . The function of this vital constitutional provision is to protect those accused of crime against possible delay, caused either by willful oppression, or the neglect of the state or its officers." (*Jones v. Superior Court* (1970) 3 Cal. 3rd 734, 738)

The California Constitution provides that an "accused" shall enjoy the right to a speedy trial. Our Supreme Court has held that a defendant becomes an "accused" when the complaint or indictment is filed. (*People v. Martinez* (2000) 22 Cal. 4th 750, 767).

The delay in the instant case is excessive and was avoidable. After the Complaint was filed and a warrant was issued, there appear to have been no reasonable steps taken to move the matter forward.

IT IS IMMATERIAL WHETHER A DELAY IN PROSECUTING A CASE IS NEGLIGENT OR PURPOSEFUL

Evidence of deprivation of due process sufficient to warrant dismissal does not require a showing of purposeful delay by the prosecution. Prejudicial delay caused by negligence of law enforcement agencies or by the prosecution is sufficient to deny a defendant the right to due process. (*Scherling v. Superior Court* (1978) 22 Cal. 3rd 493, 507; *Penney v. Superior Court* (1972) 28 Cal. App. 3rd 941, 953).

Even if the delay is merely the result of administrative malfeasance or simple negligence on the part of the state or its officers, it is clear that there must, nonetheless, be a dismissal. (*Barker v. Wingo* (1972) 407 U.S. 514).

AN UNJUSTIFIED DELAY IN ARRESTING DEFENDANT CONSTITUTES A VIOLATION OF THE DUE PROCESS IF THAT DELAY PREJUDICES THE DEFENDANT'S ABILITY TO DEFEND HIMSELF

Delay prior to the arrest of a defendant may give rise to a due process claim under the Fifth Amendment. (*U. S. v. Lovasco* (1977) 431 U.S. 783, 788-789). The court in *Scherling v. Superior Court* (1978) 22 Cal. 3rd 493, 507, held that even an unintentional delay can be the basis of a denial of a defendant's due process rights:

> We do not intend to imply that only a deliberate delay by the prosecution for the purpose of prejudicing the defense may justify a conclusion that a defendant has been deprived of due process. The ultimate inquiry in determining a claim based upon due process is whether the defendant will be denied a fair trial. If such deprivation results from unjustified delay by the prosecution coupled with prejudice, it makes no difference whether the delay was deliberately designed to disadvantage the defendant, or

whether it was caused by negligence of law enforcement agencies or the prosecution. In both situations, the defendant will be denied his right to a fair trial as a result of government conduct. [Citation omitted.] Thus, although delay may have been caused only by the negligence of the government, the prejudice suffered by a defendant may be sufficient when balanced against the reasons for the delay to constitute a denial of due process.

If not intentional, the delay in this case was, at a minimum, caused by negligence, and Defendant was prejudiced by the delay. During the extensive delay, Defendant continued to reside openly and notoriously thereafter, but law enforcement did not choose to pursue or arrest him. During that time, Defendant resided in Kern County and he could have easily been located should the Prosecution wish to pursue the charges against him.

Had Defendant's prosecution proceeded with haste he could have possibly presented evidence to prove that he was not the driver of the vehicle (which was found parked), presented evidence to disprove the offense (such as testimony as to his level of sobriety), or presented other such exculpatory evidence. However, such evidence has been lost, or at least deteriorated, by the passage of time.

In *People v. Hill* (1984) 37 Cal. 3rd 491, the Supreme Court stated that fading memories of prosecution witnesses that prevent adequate cross-examination on a material issue may constitute sufficient prejudice to warrant a finding of denial of due process. Likewise, in *Ibarra v. Municipal Court* (1984) 162 Cal. App. 3rd 853, the Court of Appeal stated that the fading memory of the defendant must be considered by the court in determining prejudice.

In *Doggett v. U.S.* (1992) 505 U.S. 647, the United States Supreme Court examined the cognizable categories of prejudice that could result to the defendant:

> We have observed in prior cases that unreasonable delay between formal accusation and trial threatens to produce more than one sort of harm, including… "the possibility that the [accused's] defense will be impaired" by dimming memories and loss of exculpatory evidence. . .. Of these forms of prejudice, "the most serious is the last, because the inability of a defendant adequately to prepare his case skews the fairness of the entire system."

As our Supreme Court explained in *Jones v. Superior Court* (1970) 3 Cal. 3rd 734, 740:

> Petitioner was clearly prejudiced. The most obvious prejudicial effect of the long pre-arrest delay was to seriously impair his ability to recall and to secure evidence of his activities at the time of the events in question. Delaying the arrest of the accused may hinder his ability to recall or reconstruct his whereabouts at the time the alleged offense occur.

In misdemeanor cases, prejudice must be presumed for delay more than a year and dismissal is required without any further showing (*Serna v. Superior Court* (1985) 40 Cal. 3rd 239, 252; see also *Stabio v. Superior Court* (1994) 21 Cal. App. 4th 1488).

EVEN MINIMAL PREJUDICE MUST BE BALANCED AGAINST THE JUSTIFICATION FOR THE DELAY

Even if the prejudice to the Defendant appears to be minimal, the court must conduct a hearing to balance the prejudice against the justification for the delay. (*Garcia v. Superior Court* (1984) 163 Cal. App. 3rd 148 (1984); *Ibarra v. Municipal Court* (1984) 162 Cal. App. 3rd 853).

In the instant case, there appears to be no reason for the extended delay. The Prosecution simply did not take actions to move the matter forward.

∞◊∞◊∞

It is no secret that the United States has staggering prosecution rates. One study suggests that one in twenty Americans will be prosecuted compared to less than one in a thousand for residents of countries such as France, Mexico, and Burma[5].

These high numbers lead to many defendants getting lost in the system with charges being filed but not moving forward. This gives rise to a motion to dismiss for delay in prosecution.

---

[5] See http://www.nationmaster.com/country-info/stats/Crime/Adults-prosecuted-per-1000

18. Set Motions Date

Some courts require that motions concerning the merits of the case be heard on a certain date, known as a Motions Date. Other courts allow the parties to file motions on regularly set dates, e.g. "criminal motions will be heard Tuesday through Thursday at 8:30 in Department LM." Still other courts require the parties to clear motions with the clerk before adding them to the motions calendar, i.e. the defense will call the clerk to determine what dates are available. If the court uses the Motions Date system, the court will generally set the first Motions Date, but if additional motions are required, the defense may be required to bring a motion to set a Motions Date.

Bill Slocumb
1929 Truxtun Ave, Ste. C
Bakersfield, CA 93301
(661)324-1400

Attorney for Donny Dave

IN THE SUPERIOR COURT OF THE STATE OF CALIFORNIA,

IN AND FOR THE COUNTY OF KERN

People of the State of California,	CASE NO. 123456
Plaintiffs,	MOTION TO SET MOTIONS DATE
- v. -	
Donny Dave,	DATE: October 16, 2017 TIME: 8:30 a.m. DEPT: CC
Defendant	Trial date: October 31, 2017 Readiness date: October 30, 2017

TO THE COURT AND THE DISTRICT ATTORNEY:
PLEASE TAKE NOTICE that at the date and time indicated above, or as soon thereafter as the matter can be heard in the above entitled court, the defendant will move that the Court set a Motions date.

The motion will be based on this notice of motion, the attached declaration, the memorandum of points and authorities served and filed herewith, the records on file in this action and on such oral and documentary evidence as may be presented at the hearing.

Dated:

                                        By Bill Slocumb,
                                              Attorney for Donny Dave

DECLARATION IN SUPPORT OF MOTION

I, Bill Slocumb, Attorney for Defendant, declare:

Additional motions are necessary to properly prepare this matter for trial. Specifically, discovery produced in response to previously litigated motions has revealed that the affidavit in support of the search warrant may have contained falsehoods, so a Motion to Traverse is needed.

Based on the foregoing, I respectfully request a new Motions Date.

Dated:

                                        By Bill Slocumb,
                                            Attorney for Donny Dave

POINTS, AUTHORITIES, AND ARGUMENT

Code of Civil Procedure §128, holds that "Every court shall have the power… To provide for the orderly conduct of proceedings before it… [and] To amend and control its process and orders so as to make them conform to law and justice…"

19. Joinder

Elliot Magnus
641 H Street
Bakersfield, CA 93304
(661)395-0240

Attorney for Danny Dean

IN THE SUPERIOR COURT OF THE STATE OF CALIFORNIA,

IN AND FOR THE COUNTY OF KERN

People of the State of California,	CASE NO. 123456
Plaintiffs,	DEFENDANT DEAN'S NOTICE OF JOINDER IN CARL CODEF'S MOTION TO CONTINUE READINESS
- v. -	
Danny Dean, Carl Codef,	DATE: October 16, 2017 TIME: 8:30 a.m. DEPT: 1
Defendants	
	Trial date: October 31, 2017 Readiness date: October 30, 2017

TO THE COURT, THE DISTRICT ATTORNEY, AND COUNSEL FOR CODEFENDANTS:

Comes now Defendant, Danny Dean, who hereby formally joins in Carl Codef's Motion to Continue Readiness.

Dated:

By   Elliot Magnus,
      Attorney for Danny Dean

20. Substitute Counsel (Marsden)

Name
Address
Phone

Defendant, Pro Per

IN THE SUPERIOR COURT OF THE STATE OF CALIFORNIA,

IN AND FOR THE COUNTY OF KERN

People of the State of California,	CASE NO. 123456
Plaintiffs,	DEFENDANT'S MOTION TO SUBSTITUTE COUNSEL [Marsden]
- v. -	
Don Dan,	DATE: October 16, 2017 TIME: 8:30 a.m. DEPT: 1
Defendant	
	Trial date: October 31, 2017 Readiness date: October 30, 2017

TO THE COURT, THE DISTRICT ATTORNEY, AND COUNSEL FOR DEFENDANT:

PLEASE TAKE NOTICE that at the date and time indicated above, or as soon thereafter as the matter can be heard in the above entitled court, the defendant will move the Court to substitute defense counsel or, in the alternative, to conduct an in camera hearing so that Defendant may assert other grounds for relief.

The motion will be based on this notice of motion, the memorandum of points and authorities served and filed herewith, on all the papers and records on file in this action, and on such oral and documentary evidence as may be presented at the hearing of the motion.

Dated: _____

By   Don Dan, Defendant

POINTS, AUTHORITIES, AND ARGUMENT

Defendant requests substitution of attorney based on ineffective assistance of counsel, conflict of interests, a breakdown of the attorney/client relationship, and/or because counsel and defendant have become embroiled in an irreconcilable conflict.

To safeguard the privilege against self-incrimination, as guaranteed by the United States Constitution and the Constitution of the State of California, Defendant requests an in camera hearing, or in the alternative, a hearing in the courtroom with the District Attorney or his or her representative excused, to submit additional reasons for wanting new defense counsel appointed.

"A defendant may be entitled to an order substituting appointed counsel if he shows that, in its absence, his Sixth Amendment right to the assistance of counsel would be denied or substantially impaired. The law governing a Marsden motion is well settled. When a defendant seeks to discharge his appointed counsel and substitute another attorney, and asserts inadequate representation, the trial court must permit the defendant to explain the basis of his contention and to relate specific instances of the attorney's inadequate performance. A defendant is entitled to relief if the record clearly shows that the first appointed attorney is not providing adequate representation or that defendant and counsel have become embroiled in such an irreconcilable conflict that ineffective representation is likely to result."

(*People v. Memro* (1995) 11 Cal. 4th 786, 857, internal citations and punctuation omitted.)

This Court cannot find that counsel's representation is adequate based solely on the record because not all matters related to counsel's representation are found in the record.

"When inadequate representation is alleged, the critical factual inquiry ordinarily relates to matters outside the trial record: whether the defendant had a defense which was not presented; whether trial counsel consulted sufficiently with the accused, and adequately investigated the facts and the law; whether the omissions charged to trial counsel resulted from inadequate preparation rather than from unwise choices of trial tactics and strategy." (*Brubaker v. Dickson* (9th Cir. 1962) 310 F. 2nd 30, 32.).

K. EX PARTE PLEADINGS

Introduction

> Ex parte pleadings are those pleadings that allow a party to communicate directly with the court without giving the other side prior notice.

Order Shortening Time

> This pleading is used to allow motions to be served and filed in fewer than the normally required number of days.

Removal Order

> This pleading is used to bring a witness who is in custody to court.

Motion to Appoint Expert

> It often takes an entire team to property defend a case. The defense team may include investigators, transcriptionists, medical experts, DNA experts, or other types of experts. This pleading is used to obtain funding for appointment of these experts.

Motion to Appoint Paralegal

> This pleading is used to obtain funding for appointment of a paralegal. The Motion to Appoint Expert shown above may also be used to appoint a paralegal, but this motion has a section explaining the special value of having a paralegal.

∞◊∞◊∞

> In order that punishment should not be an act of violence perpetrated by one or many upon a private citizen, it is essential that it should be public, speedy, necessary, the minimum possible in the given circumstances, proportionate to the crime, and determined by the law.

~Cesare Beccaria

L. SAMPLE EX PARTE PLEADINGS

1. Order Shortening Time

David Faulkner
422 Truxtun Ave
Bakersfield, CA 93301
(661)324-4777

Attorney for Danny Dean

IN THE SUPERIOR COURT OF THE STATE OF CALIFORNIA,

IN AND FOR THE COUNTY OF KERN

People of the State of California,	CASE NO. 123456
Plaintiffs,	REQUEST FOR ORDER SHORTENING
- v. -	TIME FOR SERVICE OF MOTION
Danny Dean,	DATE: October 16, 2017
Defendant	TIME: 8:30 a.m.
	DEPT: 1
	Trial date: October 31, 2017
	Readiness date: October 30, 2017

In support of this request for an order shortening time, I, David Faulkner, declare:

Due to delays in receiving the reporter's transcript, the attached motion was not prepared in time for timely filing, an Order Shortening Time is therefore necessary to file the motion so that it may be heard on October 16, 2017.

Dated:

            By David Faulkner,
               Attorney for Danny Dean

David Faulkner
422 Truxtun Ave
Bakersfield, CA 93301
(661)324-4777

Attorney for Danny Dean

IN THE SUPERIOR COURT OF THE STATE OF CALIFORNIA,

IN AND FOR THE COUNTY OF KERN

People of the State of California,	CASE NO. 123456
Plaintiffs,	ORDER SHORTENING TIME FOR SERVICE OF MOTION
- v. -	
Danny Dean,	DATE: October 16, 2017 TIME: 8:30 a.m.
Defendant	DEPT: 1
	Trial date: October 31, 2017 Readiness date: October 30, 2017

GOOD CAUSE APPEARING, IT IS HEREBY ORDERED that the attached motion shall be served on the District Attorney on or before October ____, 2017.

Dated:

                                              By Judge of the Superior Court

2. Removal Order

Joe Whittington
1706 Chester Ave., Suite 304
Bakersfield, CA 93301
(661)322-5833

Attorney for Danny Dean

IN THE SUPERIOR COURT OF THE STATE OF CALIFORNIA,
IN AND FOR THE COUNTY OF KERN

People of the State of California,	CASE NO. 123456
Plaintiffs,	REQUEST FOR REMOVAL OF CDCR INMATE
- v. -	
Danny Dean,	DATE: October 16, 2017 TIME: 8:30 a.m. DEPT: 1
Defendant	Trial date: October 31, 2017 Readiness date: October 30, 2017

I, Joe Whittington, declare:

I am the attorney representing the defendant in this action.

Mark Mendoza, who is confined in the Correctional Training Facility (CTF) under CDCR# P12345 is required to appear as a witness in the above entitled matter.

Therefore, I respectfully request an order directing Shawn Hatton, Acting Warden of CTF, to remove this inmate from the prison, and to deliver the inmate into custody of the sheriff of this county.

Further, that the sheriff of this county be ordered to deliver this inmate to Department One of the above court on October 16, 2017, at the hour of 8:30 a.m., and at such times thereafter until the inmate's testimony has concluded, and thereafter to return said prisoner to custody of Shawn Hatton, Acting Warden of CTF.

Dated:

By Joe Whittington,
Attorney for Danny Dean

Joe Whittington
1706 Chester Ave., Suite 304
Bakersfield, CA 93301
(661)322-5833

Attorney for Danny Dean

IN THE SUPERIOR COURT OF THE STATE OF CALIFORNIA,

IN AND FOR THE COUNTY OF KERN

People of the State of California, Plaintiffs, - v. - Danny Dean, Defendant	CASE NO. 123456 ORDER FOR REMOVAL OF CDCR INMATE DATE: October 16, 2017 TIME: 8:30 a.m. DEPT: 1 Trial date: October 31, 2017 Readiness date: October 30, 2017

To: Shawn Hatton, Acting Warden of CTF:

An order having been made this day by me, that Mark Mendoza, who is confined in the Correctional Training Facility (CTF) under CDCR# P12345 be produced in this court to appear as a witness, you are commanded to deliver Mark Mendoza into the custody of Donny Youngblood, Sheriff of Kern County.

Dated:

                                        By Judge of the Superior Court

3. Motion to Appoint Expert

Bill Slocumb
1929 Truxtun Ave, Ste. C
Bakersfield, CA 93301
(661)324-1400

Attorney for Danny Dean

IN THE SUPERIOR COURT OF THE STATE OF CALIFORNIA,
IN AND FOR THE COUNTY OF KERN

People of the State of California,	CASE NO. 123456
Plaintiffs,	DEFENDANT'S MOTION FOR APPOINTMENT OF PSYCHOLOGIST DR. INYO HEAD TO EXAMINE DEFENDANT (*Evidence Code §730*)
- v. -	
Danny Dean,	
Defendant	

TO THE ABOVE-ENTITLED COURT:

    Defendant hereby moves the court for an order appointing Dr. Inyo Head at the expense of the county, to examine and advise the defendant on a confidential basis, and to testify on the defendant's behalf and for such other relief as may seem just and proper to the court.

    The motion is made on the grounds that a mental health examination of the defendant and expert testimony is necessary to the preparation of the defense of this action.

    The motion is based on this notice of motion, on the attached declaration, and the memorandum of points and authorities served and filed herewith, on such supplemental declarations, affidavits, memoranda of points and authorities as may hereafter be filed with the court, on all the papers and records on file in this action, and on such oral and documentary evidence as may be presented at the hearing of the motion.
Dated:

                                      By   Bill Slocumb,
                                                  Attorney for Danny Dean

POINTS AND AUTHORITIES

THE DUE PROCESS OF EFFECTIVE COUNSEL INCLUDE THE RIGHT TO THE ANCILLARY SERVICES FOR THE PREPARATION OF THE DEFENSE

Supreme Court decisions mandate that effective assistance of counsel "… requires, when necessary, the allowance of investigative expenses or appointment of investigative assistance for indigent defendants in order to insure effective preparation of their defense by their attorneys." *(Mason v. State of Arizona* (9th Cir. 1974) 504 F. 2nd 1345, 1351).

"The due process right of effective counsel includes the right to the ancillary services necessary in the preparation of a defense. [citations omitted.] The right is codified in Penal Code section 987.2 which provides that counsel appointed for an indigent defendant shall not only be compensated by a reasonable fee but also shall be reimbursed for his necessary expense." (*People v. Faxel* (1979) 91 Cal App 3rd 327, 330)

"The Sixth Amendment right to counsel is a meaningless gesture if counsel for an indigent is denied the use of working tools essential to the establishment of what would appear to be a tenable or possible defense." (*People v. Gunnerson*, 74 Cal App 3rd 370, 379).

It cannot be doubted that the right to counsel guaranteed by both the federal and state Constitutions includes, and indeed presumes, the right to effective counsel, and "the right to effective counsel also includes the right to ancillary services necessary in the preparation of a defense." (*Keenan v, Superior Court* (1982) 31 Cal 3rd 424, 428) "A fundamental part of the constitutional right of an accused to be represented by counsel is that his attorney…is obviously entitled to the aid of such expert assistance as he may need…in preparing the defense." (*Re Ketchel* (1968) 68 Cal 2nd 397, 399-400)

THE RIGHT TO SUCH COURT-ORDERED SERVICES IS SUPPORTED BY STATUTE

Evidence Code §730 explicitly provides for court-appointed experts:

> When it appears to the court, at any time before or during the trial of an action, that expert evidence is or may be required by the court or by any party to the action, the court on its own motion or on motion of any party may appoint one or more

experts to investigate, to render a report as may be ordered by the court, and to testify as an expert at the trial of the action relative to the fact or matter as to which such expert evidence is or may be required. The court may fix the compensation for such services, if any, rendered by any person appointed under this section, in addition to any services as a witness, at such amount as seems reasonable to the court.

Evidence Code §731(a) and *Government Code §29603* clearly state that the county must pay those court-ordered expenses.

These statutes do not enumerate the type of experts to be appointed, but the Supreme Court has held that "the right to such services is to be inferred from at least two statutes respecting an indigent defendant's right to legal assistance." (*Corenevsky v. Superior Court* (1984) 36 Cal 3rd 307, 319)

THE RIGHT TO COUNSEL INCLUDES THE RIGHT TO HAVE ANY COMMUNICATION MADE TO EXPERTS REMAIN CONFIDENTIAL

The Court of Appeal has held that the right to counsel guaranteed by the Sixth Amendment to the United States Constitution "also includes the right to have any communications made to experts remain confidential." (*Torres v. Municipal Court for Los Angeles Judicial Dist.* (1975) 50 Cal App 3rd 778, 784).

∞◊∞◊∞

Some courts have a list of approved mental health professionals and/or other experts. In these courts, a request for appointment of a mental health expert to examine the defendant may result in an expert from the approved list being randomly chosen to examine the defendant.

The same mental health expert may be called upon to determine whether the defendant is competent to stand trial and whether the defendant was insane at the time of the offense.

Convincing a jury that a defendant is not guilty by reason of insanity doesn't mean the defendant gets off. It usually means that the defendant simply serves his sentence in a mental institution, which may sometimes be a longer sentence than what would have been served if sentenced to prison.

DECLARATION IN SUPPORT OF MOTION TO APPOINT MENTAL HEALTH EXPERT

I, Bill Slocumb, Attorney for Defendant, declare and aver as follows:

1. Defendant is charged, inter alia, with first degree murder. He is facing a life sentence.
2. I am informed and believe that Defendant is indigent in that this assignment came to me as a Public Defender conflict, and Defendant is currently in custody.
3. Defendant has entered a plea of Not Guilty By Reason of Insanity. I request the appointment of Dr. Inyo Head, whose C.V. is attached, for the purpose of examining Defendant.
4. The Prosecution has their own mental health professional, who is scheduled to examine Defendant.
5. Dr. Head's fee for reviewing the massive amount of discovery is $3,750.00 for 25 hours of work at a rate of $150.00 per hour.
6. An additional flat rate of $1,500.00 is needed for travel time from Oxnard to Bakersfield and back, examination of defendant, and consult with attorney regarding examination.
7. As such, counsel is requesting that Dr. Head be appointed for the initial fee of $5,250.00.

Dated:

By   Bill Slocumb,
      Attorney for Danny Dean

∞◊∞◊∞

By "justice", I understand nothing more than that bond which is necessary to keep the interest of individuals united, without which men would return to their original state of barbarity. All punishments which exceed the necessity of preserving this bond are, in their nature, unjust.

~Cesare Beccaria

Bill Slocumb
1929 Truxtun Ave, Ste. C
Bakersfield, CA 93301
(661)324-1400

Attorney for Danny Dean

IN THE SUPERIOR COURT OF THE STATE OF CALIFORNIA,

IN AND FOR THE COUNTY OF KERN

People of the State of California,	CASE NO. 123456
Plaintiffs,	ORDER APPOINTING PSYCHOLOGIST TO EXAMINE DEFENDANT
- v. -	*(Evidence Code §730)*
Danny Dean,	
Defendant	

Pursuant to Defendant's Ex Parte application, IT IS HEREBY ORDERED that Dr. Inyo Head is appointed to assist the Defense as a psychologist and that a maximum of $5,250.00, be authorized for Dr. Head for work to be performed at a rate of $150.00 per hour.

Dated:

_____
By   Judge of the Superior Court

∞◊∞◊∞

Some defendants have refused to cooperate with mental health experts under the expectation that the expert cannot find the defendant competent to stand trial unless the expert examines the defendant. This usually results in the expert making a finding that the defendant is "malingering" and the defendant is declared to be competent. This can make the defendant look bad in the eyes of the court. It is generally best to cooperate with the defense team, including any mental health experts.

4. Motion to Appoint Paralegal

Larry Fields
2112 17th St
Bakersfield, CA 93301
(661)861-9750

Attorney for Danny Dean

IN THE SUPERIOR COURT OF THE STATE OF CALIFORNIA,
IN AND FOR THE COUNTY OF KERN

People of the State of California,	CASE NO. 123456
Plaintiffs,	CONFIDENTIAL EX PARTE APPLICATION FOR ORDER APPOINTING PARALEGAL (*Evidence Code §730*)
- v. -	
Danny Dean,	
Defendant	

TO THE ABOVE-ENTITLED COURT:
    Defendant requests an order appointing Victor VeVea as a paralegal at the expense of the county to assist the defendant on a confidential basis and for such other orders as may seem just and proper to the court.

    This request is made on the grounds that the assistance of this paralegal is necessary to the preparation of the defense of this action.

    This request is based on the attached declaration, on the memorandum of points and authorities served and filed herewith, on such supplemental declarations, affidavits, or memorandum of points and authorities as may hereafter be filed with the court, on all the papers and records on file in this action, and on such further oral and documentary evidence as may be presented at the hearing of this request.
Dated:

                                        By Larry Fields,
                                               Attorney for Danny Dean

POINTS AND AUTHORITIES

THE DUE PROCESS OF EFFECTIVE COUNSEL INCLUDES THE RIGHT TO THE ANCILLARY SERVICES FOR THE PREPARATION OF THE DEFENSE

Supreme Court decisions mandate that effective assistance of counsel "... requires, when necessary, the allowance of investigative expenses or appointment of investigative assistance for indigent defendants in order to insure effective preparation of their defense by their attorneys." *(Mason v. State of Arizona* (9th Cir. 1974) 504 F. 2nd 1345, 1351).

"The due process right of effective counsel includes the right to the ancillary services necessary in the preparation of a defense. [Citations omitted.] The right is codified in Penal Code section 987.2 which provides that counsel appointed for an indigent defendant shall not only be compensated by a reasonable fee but also shall be reimbursed for his necessary expense." (*People v. Faxel* (1979) 91 Cal App 3rd 327, 330)

"The Sixth Amendment right to counsel is a meaningless gesture if counsel for an indigent is denied the use of working tools essential to the establishment of what would appear to be a tenable or possible defense." (*People v. Gunnerson*, 74 Cal App 3rd 370, 379).

It cannot be doubted that the right to counsel guaranteed by both the federal and state Constitutions includes, and indeed presumes, the right to effective counsel, and "the right to effective counsel also includes the right to ancillary services necessary in the preparation of a defense." (*Keenan v, Superior Court* (1982) 31 Cal 3rd 424, 428) "A fundamental part of the constitutional right of an accused to be represented by counsel is that his attorney…is obviously entitled to the aid of such expert assistance as he may need…in preparing the defense." (*Re Ketchel* (1968) 68 Cal 2nd 397, 399-400)

PARALEGAL SERVICES ARE REASONABLY NECESSARY

"In the modern world of legal practice, the delegation of repetitive legal tasks to paralegals has become a necessary fixture. Such delegation has become an integral part of the struggle to keep down the costs of legal representation. Moreover, the delegation of such tasks to specialized, well-educated non-lawyers may well ensure greater accuracy…" (*Pincay v. Andrews* (2004) 389 F. 3rd 853).

Paralegals are necessary support services for attorneys (see generally, *Missouri v. Jenkins* 491 U.S. 274; *Trustees of Const. v. Redland Ins. Co.*, 460 F. 3rd 1253 (9th Cir. 2006); *Otay Ranch, L.P. v. County of San Diego* (2014) 230 Cal. App. 4th 60; *No Toxic Air, Inc. v. Lehigh Southwest Cement Company* (2016) 1 Cal. App. 5th 1136).

"[S]ecretarial and paralegal services" are "necessary support services for attorneys" (*Salton Bay Marina, Inc. v. Imperial Irrigation Dist.* (1985) 172 Cal. App. 3rd 914).

It appears to be without dispute that paralegals result in a net cost savings. It may even be improper for an attorney to complete tasks that would better be assigned to a paralegal. For example, in *Carver v. Chevron U.S.A., Inc.* (2002) 97 Cal. App. 4th 132, the trial court properly reduced payment to the attorney because the court found "that some charges could have been reduced had a paralegal performed the tasks…"

THE RIGHT TO SUCH COURT-ORDERED SERVICES IS SUPPORTED BY STATUTE

Evidence Code §730 explicitly provides for court-appointed experts:

> When it appears to the court, at any time before or during the trial of an action, that expert evidence is or may be required by the court or by any party to the action, the court on its own motion or on motion of any party may appoint one or more experts to investigate, to render a report as may be ordered by the court, and to testify as an expert at the trial of the action relative to the fact or matter as to which such expert evidence is or may be required. The court may fix the compensation for such services, if any, rendered by any person appointed under this section, in addition to any services as a witness, at such amount as seems reasonable to the court.

Evidence Code §731(a) and *Government Code §29603* clearly state that the county must pay those court-ordered expenses.

These statutes do not enumerate the type of experts to be appointed, but the Supreme Court has held that "the right to such services is to be inferred from at least two statutes respecting an indigent defendant's right to legal assistance." (*Corenevsky v. Superior Court* (1984) 36 Cal 3rd 307, 319)

THE RIGHT TO COUNSEL INCLUDES THE RIGHT TO HAVE ANY COMMUNICATION MADE TO EXPERTS REMAIN CONFIDENTIAL

The Court of Appeal has held that the right to counsel guaranteed by the Sixth Amendment to the United States Constitution "also includes the right to have any communications made to experts remain confidential." (*Torres v. Municipal Court for Los Angeles Judicial Dist.* (1975) 50 Cal App 3rd 778, 784).

∞◊∞◊∞

The American Bar Association (ABA) defines a paralegal as "a person, qualified by education, training or work experience who is employed or retained by a lawyer, law office, corporation, governmental agency or other entity and who performs specifically delegated substantive legal work for which a lawyer is responsible." *California Business and Professions Code §6450* gives a similar definition and goes on to explain the duties of a paralegal:

> Tasks performed by a paralegal include, but are not limited to, case planning, development, and management; legal research; interviewing clients; fact gathering and retrieving information; drafting and analyzing legal documents; collecting, compiling, and utilizing technical information to make an independent decision and recommendation to the supervising attorney; and representing clients before a state or federal administrative agency if that representation is permitted by statute, court rule, or administrative rule or regulation.

There are multiple tasks that a paralegal is specifically prohibited from doing, including providing legal advice, representing a client in court, and selecting pleadings for a client. All of the work done by the paralegal is under the supervision of the attorney.

The paralegal can, and will, make suggestions to the attorney as to what motions might be proper in a given case. A defendant is also free to suggest motions to the attorney, but it is the attorney who will ultimately decide the strategy of the case, which motions to file, what jury instructions to request, and what witnesses to call.

There are, however, limits to the control the attorney has over the case. As examples, only the defendant can choose whether to testify, and only the defendant can accept or reject a plea bargain.

DECLARATION IN SUPPORT OF MOTION TO APPOINT PARALEGAL

I, Larry Fields, Attorney for Defendant, declare and aver as follows:

1. Defendant is charged, inter alia, with first degree murder. He is facing a life sentence.
2. I am informed and believe that Defendant is indigent in that this assignment came to me as a Public Defender conflict, and Defendant is currently in custody.
3. The discovery in this case is voluminous. The Prosecution has produced multiple computer disks and thousands of pages of other discovery. I do not know the true extent of the electronic discovery because I have not yet fully reviewed this evidence.
4. It is not reasonable or economical for me to personally review all of the discovery in that a paralegal charges half of my billing rate – a cost that will ultimately be borne by the County.
5. I, therefore, request the appointment of Paralegal Victor VeVea to assist me.
6. I need this skilled death penalty qualified paralegal to listen to the audio files, view the video files, and otherwise sift through and sort the voluminous discovery and call to my attention important evidence.
7. For me to personally review all of this evidence, much of which I expect to be mundane or wholly irrelevant, would consume many, many hours (at a billing rate double that requested by this expert) and would divert my attention from more important tasks, such as reviewing the relevant evidence, conducting legal research, supervising experts, and otherwise preparing this case for trial.
8. Mr. VeVea's resume is attached, which also demonstrates his qualifications.
9. Mr. VeVea's billing rate is $100 per hour. I expect to need at least two fulltime weeks of his services.

Based on the foregoing, I request an initial authorization of eighty hours (80) hours at $100.00 per hour for a total of $8,000.00.

Dated:

By   Larry Fields,
      Attorney for Danny Dean

Larry Fields
2112 17th St
Bakersfield, CA 93301
(661)861-9750

Attorney for Danny Dean

IN THE SUPERIOR COURT OF THE STATE OF CALIFORNIA,

IN AND FOR THE COUNTY OF KERN

People of the State of California,	CASE NO. 123456
Plaintiffs,	ORDER APPOINTING PARALEGAL
- v. -	(*Evidence Code §730*)
Danny Dean,	
Defendant	

Pursuant to Defendant's Ex Parte application, IT IS HEREBY ORDERED that Victor VeVea is appointed to assist the Defense and that a maximum of $8,000.00 be authorized for Mr. VeVea for work to be performed at his rate of $100 per hour.

Dated:

By _____
    Judge of the Superior Court

∞◊∞◊∞

There's no way to rule innocent men. The only power any government has is the power to crack down on criminals. Well, when there aren't enough criminals, one makes them. One declares so many things to be a crime that it becomes impossible for men to live without breaking laws.

~Ayn Rand

M. TRIAL (IN LIMINE) MOTIONS

The term "limine," from the Latin *limen*, meaning "threshold," generally refers to a motion made shortly before the start of evidence in a trial.

There is no specific statutory authority for the motion in limine, but *Rules of Court, Rule 31112(f)* implicitly recognizes the motion by providing that "a motion in limine filed before or during trial need not be accompanied by a notice of hearing. The timing and place of the filing and service of the motion are at the discretion of the trial judge." Several other rules also implicitly recognize motions in limine (see *Rules 3.20, 3.670, 3.1547*, etc.).

Many issues are the proper subject of motions in limine, but the most common use of in limine motions is to prevent the jury from receiving unfavorable evidence. The court has discretion to rule on evidentiary matters before the jury has a chance to even learn of their existence (*Evidence Code §402; People v. Jennings* (1988) 46 Cal. 3rd 963).

Other proper subjects for motions in limine stem from the court's power to "Provide for the orderly conduct of proceedings before it" (*Code of Civil Procedure §128(a)(3)*) and to "Control its process and orders so as to make them conform to law and justice" (*id. §128(a)(8)*).

The court in *Kelly v. New West Federal Savings* (1996) 49 Cal. App. 4th 659 explained motions in limine:

> In recent years, the use of motions in limine has become more prevalent, primarily by defense counsel to address a number of perceived concerns. It is not uncommon for the trial court to be presented with in excess of 10 separate motions in limine...
>
> Motions in limine are a commonly used tool of trial advocacy and management in both criminal and civil cases. Such motions are generally brought at the beginning of trial, although they may also be brought during trial when evidentiary issues are anticipated by the parties. In either event, they are argued by the parties, either orally or in writing or both, and ruled upon by the trial judge. The usual purpose of motions in limine is to preclude the presentation of evidence deemed inadmissible and prejudicial by the moving party. A typical order in limine excludes the challenged evidence and directs counsel, parties, and witnesses not to refer to the excluded matters during trial. The

advantage of such motions is to avoid the obviously futile attempt to "unring the bell" in the event a motion to strike is granted in the proceedings before the jury.

Motions in limine serve other purposes as well. They permit more careful consideration of evidentiary issues than would take place in the heat of battle during trial. They minimize side-bar conferences and disruptions during trial, allowing for an uninterrupted flow of evidence. Finally, by resolving potentially critical issues at the outset, they enhance the efficiency of trials and promote settlements."

The above is taken from California Criminal Defense Motions in Limine, which contains a large collection of sample Motions in Limine. This book, however, only gives a cursory overview of Motions in Limine.

∞◊∞◊∞

It is more important that innocence be protected than it is that guilt be punished, for guilt and crimes are so frequent in this world that they cannot all be punished.

But if innocence itself is brought to the bar and condemned, perhaps to die, then the citizen will say, 'whether I do good or whether I do evil is immaterial, for innocence itself is no protection,' and if such an idea as that were to take hold in the mind of the citizen that would be the end of security whatsoever.

~John Adams, *The Portable John Adams*

N. SAMPLE TRIAL (IN LIMINE) MOTIONS

1. Omnibus Motion in Limine

Elliot Magnus
641 H Street
Bakersfield, CA 93304
(661)395-0240

Attorney for Dave Douglass

IN THE SUPERIOR COURT OF THE STATE OF CALIFORNIA,

IN AND FOR THE COUNTY OF KERN

People of the State of California,	CASE NO. 123456
Plaintiffs,	DEFENDANT'S OMNIBUS MOTIONS IN LIMINE
- v. -	
Dave Douglass,	
Defendant	

TO THE COURT AND THE PROSECUTION, PLEASE TAKE NOTICE that Defendant hereby moves the Court to issue orders on Motions in Limine as described herein:

A trial court has discretion to rule on evidentiary matters prior to their actual admission into evidence (*Evidence Code §402*; *People v. Jennings* (1988) 46 Cal 3rd 963).

In *Lemer v. Boise Cascade, Inc.* (1980) 107 Cal. App. 3rd 1, the court acknowledged that the granting of an order in limine was a reflection of the court's discretion to exclude evidence pursuant to *Evidence Code §352*.

Although not specifically referring to "motions in limine," numerous California appellate decisions have indicated that pretrial motions to exclude evidence are proper. (See as examples *Cherrigan v. City and County of San Francisco* (1968) 262 Cal. App. 2nd 643, 646; *Sacramento and San Joaquin Drainage District v. Reed* (1963) 215 Cal. App. 2nd 60, 68, modified (1964) 217

Cal. App. 2nd 611).

Evidence Code §402 allows the court to hear and determine the question of the admissibility of evidence outside the presence or hearing of the jury. (See *Mize v. Atchinson, Topeka & Santa Fe Ry. Co.* (1975) 46 Cal. App. 3rd 436, 448).

This Court has the power to "Provide for the orderly conduct of proceedings before it" (*Code of Civil Procedure §128(a)(3)*) and to "Control its process and orders so as to make them conform to law and justice" (*id. §128(a)(8)*).

Consistent with these principals, Defendant respectfully requests that the Court make use of its powers to issue rulings on the following motions in limine before jury selection begins:

1. Exclude all evidence of, and references to, the statement the defendant is alleged to have made, or in the alternative conduct a hearing pursuant to *Evidence Code §402* to evaluate the statement's admissibility.

   At the time of the statement, the defendant was in custody and did not make a knowing and intelligent waiver of his *Miranda* rights. The constitutional protections set out in *Miranda v. Arizona* 384 U.S. 436, apply not only to direct custodial interrogation but to also to police conduct which is designed to elicit an incriminating response. See *Rhode Island v. Innis* (1980) 446 U.S. 291; *Missouri v. Seibert*, 542 U.S. 600 (2004).

   Further, the admission of evidence of the defendant's statement would violate the defendant's rights under the *United States and California Constitutions*. The defense requests a hearing to determine whether the alleged admissions were in fact voluntary or as the result of the undue coercion of a person who was wounded and under arrest.

2. To exclude any pretrial statements made until the "corpus delicti" requirement is met (*People v. Cullen* (1951) 37 Cal. 2nd 614, 624.)

3. The defense requests that no witness be allowed to testify as an expert, unless and until such time as defense is given prior notice of its intent, and to do so in full compliance with the discovery statute and court rules. That all matters related to the issue of witnesses be argue outside the presence of the jury and on the record.

4. That the prosecutor be admonished not to display any identification, badges that appear to identify him as law enforcement, as the mere display of said paraphernalia is intended to argue his own arguable importance in the eyes of the jury. Such display serves no other purpose, and this prosecutor's use of said devices is unique and pervasive.

5. That the prosecutor not be permitted to use the voir dire process to influence the jury in the case, with information specifically directed to influence the jury. This would include references to the recent events in California involving the shooting of police officers.

6. That the prosecutor not be permitted to use the booking photographs of the defendants on the front of his "trial binders" in order to create the image that the defendants' are in custody, are dangerous criminals. The use of the items described is an argument without any evidentiary value, and more suited for argument than for the subtle attempt to influence the jury.

7. That the prosecutor not be permitted to open the gate to the jurors as they enter and exit the courtroom. The act itself is a manner of communication which should be foreclosed as it is an impermissible communication between the government and the people, which serves no other purpose than that of influencing the jury.

8. That the prosecutor not be permitted to use computer images that serve as a leading question in the context of the presentation of evidence on direct. The prosecutor has in the past used computer enhanced graphics to "walk through" his witnesses' testimony.

9. That the prosecutor not be permitted to use photographic displays in order to show the prevalence of "gang culture." In the past he has displayed such photographs showing police action in what appears to be minority citizens arrested without cause by the police. This is an impermissible argument, that appeals to the bias and fears of the jury.

10. That the defense be permitted to photograph the evidence to be admitted into evidence by the prosecution in order to protect its integrity and the possibility of tampering of those items.

11. That the prosecutor be admonished to treat with respect and with the decorum proper of a court of law of all witnesses, particularly defense witnesses.

12. To order all witnesses not to talk or otherwise communicate with each other or others, except the District Attorney and Defense Counsel and their respective investigators, until the completion of the trial regarding matters pertaining to their testimony.

13. Permit defense counsel (and the Prosecution if it wishes) to bring or otherwise make any challenges for cause at sidebar.

14. Exclude all trial witnesses from the courtroom, until and except while testifying.

15. Order that witnesses, including law enforcement, be prohibited from discussing the testimony to be proffered in this case, within the presence of jurors and other witnesses.

16. Require the prosecution to advise its witnesses, particularly law enforcement witnesses, of the Court's rulings regarding the In Limine motions and of pending evidentiary matters not yet ruled by the court.

17. Order that all In Limine Rulings remain in full force and effect for the duration of the Trial; unless they are reserved by the court and then only until such time as the court rule on the said motions.

Date:

_____

Elliot Magnus,
Attorney for Defendant

∞◊∞◊∞

Elliot Explains:

  Motions in Limine may be brought orally, in a list like the one above, or in individual written motions. Oral motions are often granted or denied quickly without much discussion. When submitting a list of motions, such as the one above, judges will often rule in groups without giving counsel much opportunity to argue. For example, a judge might say something like, "Motion one is denied. Two through four are granted. Five is denied. Let's talk about number six." A discussion of prejudicial evidence (Motion One) is often an essential motion. One way to slow down the process and get the court to discuss individual motions in limine is to file and argue each motion separately.

  ~Attorney Elliot Magnus (661)395-0240

2. Motion in Limine to Exclude Prejudicial Evidence

Evidence Code §352 is one of the primary code sections used in Motions in Limine. It allows for the exclusion of prejudicial evidence, but only if that evidence is not significantly relative or important to the case.

Larry Fields
2112 17th St
Bakersfield, CA 93301
(661)861-9750

Attorney for Dave Douglass

IN THE SUPERIOR COURT OF THE STATE OF CALIFORNIA,

IN AND FOR THE COUNTY OF KERN

People of the State of California,	CASE NO. 123456
Plaintiffs,	MOTIONS IN LIMINE TO EXCLUDE PREJUDICIAL
- v. -	EVIDENCE
Dave Douglass,	
Defendant	

TO THE COURT AND THE PROSECUTION, PLEASE TAKE NOTICE that Defendant moves the Court for an order prohibiting the Prosecution from directly or indirectly using, mentioning, or attempting to convey to the jury in any manner any evidence concerning [insert prejudicial evidence here].

Date:

              _____
              Larry Fields,
              Attorney for Defendant

POINTS, AUTHORITIES, AND ARGUMENT

By this Motion in Limine, Defendant seeks to enjoin the Prosecution from introducing evidence concerning [insert prejudicial evidence here. Examples of prejudicial evidence could be matters such as defendant's prior misdemeanor convictions, defendant's religion or sexuality, police statements to defendant, defendant's exercise of right to counsel, etc.]

Examples of the way the Prosecution might attempt to inform the jury about [prejudicial evidence] include:
1. References to the fact that law enforcement knew about [the evidence].
2. Evidence indicating that a witness changed his conduct or opinion based on [the evidence].
3. Questions directed to the Defendant about [the evidence.]

The probative value of such evidence is far outweighed by the potential for undue prejudice caused by its admissibility. The inflammatory nature of [the prejudicial evidence] would unduly prejudice Defendant, and that evidence will give the appearance that Defendant and/or the witnesses testifying on his behalf have the proclivity towards criminal behavior that leads to the conduct alleged against Defendant.

Evidence Code §352 states "The court in its discretion may exclude evidence if its probative value is substantially outweighed by the probability that its admission will (a) necessitate undue consumption of time or (b) create substantial danger of undue prejudice, of confusing the issues, or of misleading the jury."

Prejudicial impeachment evidence should be excluded (see *People v. Beagle* (1972) 6 Cal. 3rd 441, 452-53 [felony conviction evidence may be excluded where the probative value is outweighed by the danger of undue prejudice])

The Prosecution does not have a need for [the prejudicial evidence] in order to prove any of the current charges. The Prosecution may argue that they should be allowed to introduce such evidence to prove malice, common design or plan, knowledge of the nature of contraband, or for impeachment, but such evidence is not relevant.

Should the Court determine the need to make reference to any facts related to [the prejudicial evidence], such evidence should not be presented in such a way that it informs the jury of [the prejudicial evidence].

3. Motion in Limine to Federalize Objections

Elliot Magnus
641 H Street
Bakersfield, CA 93304
(661)395-0240
Attorney for Dave Douglass

IN THE SUPERIOR COURT OF THE STATE OF CALIFORNIA,
IN AND FOR THE COUNTY OF KERN

People of the State of California,	CASE NO. 123456
Plaintiffs,	MOTIONS IN LIMINE TO FEDERALIZE OBJECTIONS
- v. -	
Dave Douglass,	
Defendant	

TO THE COURT AND THE PROSECUTION, PLEASE TAKE NOTICE that Defendant moves the Court for an order permitting shorthand objections to federalize objections instead of lengthy, record-making objections.

Date:

             Elliot Magnus,
             Attorney for Defendant

∞◊∞◊∞

Elliot Explains:

 The federal courts only apply federal law when reviewing a conviction. Therefore, if objections are only made based on state grounds, the federal court may consider that federal constitutional objections have been waived. This could result in a conviction being affirmed by a federal court without review on the merits of the case.

    ~ Attorney Elliot Magnus (661)395-0240

POINTS, AUTHORITIES, AND ARGUMENT

Objections Must Be "Federalized" To Preserve Error

To make a proper constitutional objection, the state and federal courts have required precision and specificity by counsel. In other words, simply objecting "hearsay," will not preserve a Sixth Amendment confrontation issue, nor will objecting "352" or "unfair trial" preserve a due process issue.

For example, in *Duncan v. Henry* (1995) 513 U.S. 364, Mr. Henry was tried in a California court for allegedly molesting a five year old child. The prosecution was allowed to put on evidence of the parent of another child who testified that twenty years previous, Henry molested that child. Henry's lawyer objected that the evidence should not come in and cited *Evidence Code §352*, arguing the evidence was far more unduly prejudicial than relevant. The parent testified and Mr. Henry was convicted. On direct appeal, his lawyers argued that the evidence was irrelevant and inflammatory and that the resulting error caused a miscarriage of justice under the California Constitution (the standard for whether an error is harmless under the state constitution). The Court of Appeal found error, but ruled it harmless.

Mr. Henry then petitioned in federal district court, arguing that the error was not harmless and denied him federal due process of law. The district court granted the petition, and the Court of Appeal for the Ninth Circuit affirmed the ruling, but the U.S. Supreme Court summarily reversed the grant of relief stating that Mr. Henry never explicitly raised the federal due process issue in state court and thus did not "exhaust" his claim. The court observed that the test for the state law claim was similar to, but not quite the same as, the federal due process claim. By not intoning the magic words "due process under the federal constitution," the issue was lost and Mr. Henry's reversal of his felony conviction was lost with it.

As the Supreme Court stated, similarity of claims is not enough to exhaust an issue in state court to permit its being raised in federal court. Justice Steven's dissent placed the impact of this ruling more bluntly: the case "tightens the pleading screws ... to hold that the exhaustion doctrine includes an exact labeling requirement." (*Duncan v. Henry* (1995) 513 U.S. 364, 368.)

In *Idaho v. Wright* (1990) 497 U.S. 805, 812, two codefendants were convicted of child molestation and each appealed. One, Mr. Giles, appealed only on statutory hearsay grounds. The second, Ms. Wright, raised hearsay and the related constitutional Confrontation issue. The Idaho Supreme Court rejected Mr. Giles's argument and affirmed his conviction, but it agreed with Ms. Wright on her Confrontation claim and reversed her convictions. The ruling as to Ms. Wright was affirmed by the U.S. Supreme Court. Not federalizing his claim cost Mr. Giles a reversal of his conviction.

In *Baldwin v. Reese* (2004) 541 U.S. 27, the court held that the petitioner did not "fairly present" claim of ineffective assistance of appellate counsel to the state courts when his briefs in the state court did not complain that the ineffective assistance violated federal law. Just stating that the claim violates "due process" does not raise a federal claim. (*Shumway v. Payne* (9th Cir. 2000) 223 F. 3rd 982, 987-988 [petitioner "had to alert the state courts to the fact that [she] was asserting a claim under the United States Constitution"].)

Of course, the federal rules apply equally to state review: no objection on appropriate grounds, no review on appeal because the issue has not been preserved. (*People v. Clark* (1993) 5 Cal. 4th 950, 988 n. 13 [When a party does not raise an argument at trial, he may not do so on appeal]; see also *In re Robbins* (1998) 18 Cal. 4th 770; *People v. Gordon* (1990) 50 Cal. 3rd 1223, 1254, n. 6 [a hearsay objection does not raise a federal confrontation question and thus the federal constitutional issue was waived by counsel's incompetently made objection]; *People v. Raley* (1992) 2 Cal. 4th 870, 892 [defendant contended on appeal the court erred in admitting evidence and violated his federal constitutional rights, but because defendant objected only on statutory grounds at trial, the constitutional arguments are not cognizable on appeal].)

This is no small point. Precious constitutional rights can be sacrificed for lack of the utterance of a few syllables in stating an objection. (See, e.g, *Peterson v. Lampert* (9th Cir. 2003) 319 F. 3rd 1153 [petitioner did not fairly present his federal claim to state supreme court because on the face of his petition for review he expressly limited his claim to state constitutional law, used the term "inadequate" assistance instead of "ineffective" assistance, and cited only state law cases – federal petition dismissed as a result].) Accord *Hiivala v. Wood* (9th Cir. 1999) 195 F. 3rd 1098, 1106 (holding that, when the petitioner failed to cite federal case law or mention the federal Constitution in his state court briefing, he did not alert the state court to the federal nature of his claims).

If there is an appeal of the instant matter, the state will undoubtedly urge that trial counsel waived raising a constitutional claim and thus the defendant must be deemed procedurally barred from asserting it – "[t]ime and again in his briefs, [the State Attorney General] claims that a contention by defendant is procedurally barred." (*People v. Gordon* (1990) 50 Cal. 3rd 1223, 1250.)

Proposed Remedies

To save this court's time during this trial, to not frustrate the jury during needless record-making sidebars for the utterance of lengthy grounds for objections, and to not unduly interrupt opposing counsel's presentation of his or her case, counsel requests permission to use abbreviated terminology in making his constitutional objections. This same simplified technique is commonly used to make standard evidentiary objections under the *Evidence Code*. Thus, it is common to object by saying "*352*" in order to make an objection to evidence which has some relevance but which is outweighed by its prejudicial value. By the same token, the defense requests to make his constitutional objections in the following manner.

Option #1: The simplest alternative would be to make every hearsay, relevance or "352" objection deemed to have been made under the due process clause of the 14th Amendment, and under the confrontation clause of the 6th and 14th Amendments. (This requires agreement by the court on the record.)

Option #2: If option #1 is rejected, then a "by the numbers" alternative is proposed: Any 5th Amendment due process objection would be made by simply by adding "Fifth" to the evidentiary objection. Sixth Amendment confrontation or right to present evidence issues would be made by adding "Sixth" to such claim protected by the 6th Amendment. When objecting to unconstitutional argument by the prosecutor to the jury, counsel would object by saying "prosecution error." This too requires agreement by the court on the record.

The specifics of incorporated meaning of either option #1 or #2 are as follows:

"Fifth" means Fifth Amendment Due Process Clause:

> This objection encompasses the Fifth Amendment of the U.S. Constitution due process guarantee of a fair trial as made available to the States through the 14th Amendment.

"Sixth" means Sixth Amendment Confrontation and Right to Present Evidence in Defense of the Accused:

> This objection states that the defendant's state and federal constitutional rights to confront witnesses against him as guaranteed by the *Sixth and Fourteenth Amendments* to the United States Constitution, and under the similar, but separate and independent California Constitutional protections provided by *article one, sections seven and fifteen* are violated.

"Prosecution Error" means the following:

> This objection includes the statement that the prosecutor's comment is irrelevant, inflammatory, and prejudicial. The objection is grounded in the defendant's state and federal due process rights to a fair trial under the *Fifth and Fourteenth Amendments* to the United States Constitution, as well as defendant's state and federal constitutional right to confront witnesses against him as guaranteed by the *Sixth and Fourteenth* Amendments to the United States Constitution, and under the similar, but separate and independent California Constitutional protections provided by *article one, sections seven and fifteen*.

> When this objection is made, Defendant also asks the Court to assign this as misconduct, strike the offending comments, and admonish the jury to disregard it per *People v. Bolton* (1979) 23 Cal. 3rd 208, 215-16, n. 5. Counsel requests the following wording for the admonition:

>> Ladies and Gentlemen of the jury, the prosecutor has just made certain uncalled for insinuations about the defendant. I want you to know that the prosecutor has absolutely no evidence to present to you to back up these insinuations. The prosecutor's improper remarks amount to an attempt to prejudice you against the defendant. Were you to believe these unwarranted insinuations, and convict the defendant on the basis of them, I would have to declare a mistrial. Therefore, you must disregard these improper, unsupported remarks.

O. OBJECTIONS

More than a hundred possible objections can be thought up based on statutes, rules, and court decisions, but most of these objections rarely come up and have enough of an overlap with other objections that detailed knowledge of obscure objections is not needed.

A few obscure objections are presented here for entertainment:
- Bickerstaff – objection to the argument that defendant is probably guilty.
- Doyle – objection to comments on the defendant's exercise of the right to remain silent (sometimes called Griffin objection).
- Falconer – objection to argument that a defendant should be found guilty of manslaughter prior to determining whether defendant is guilty of the murder of the same person.
- Bain – objection to the prosecutor giving his personal opinion that the defendant is guilty.

If an objection is sustained after the witness has already answered the question, the court may "strike" the answer and "admonish" the jury to disregard the answer. To admonish, the court tells the jury something like, "you are to disregard the answer to that question."

Some of the more common objections at trial include:

Relevance

Evidence must be relevant. Evidence is relevant when it tends to prove or disprove a fact of consequence. (*Evidence Code §§210, 350, and 351.*)

352

A trial judge may exclude relevant evidence if its probative value is substantially outweighed by its prejudicial effect. Evidence is prejudicial if it may bias the jury, confuse the jury, waste time, or unduly delay the proceeding. (*Evidence Code §352.*)

Facts Not in Evidence

A question may not assume as true a fact that has not yet been introduced in evidence. For example, "when did you leave the crime scene?" assumes that the person was at a particular location and that a crime has been committed.

Foundation

Closely related to Facts Not in Evidence, and sometimes interchangeable, is a foundation objection. An attorney cannot ask the witness to answer a question that lacks foundation. "What did you see defendant do?" lacks foundation unless it is first established that the witness was present and could see something. (*Evidence Code §400, et seq.*)

Hearsay

Hearsay is a statement made other than when the person is testifying that is offered for the truth of the matter stated. Hearsay is generally not admissible, but there are many exceptions. Also, an out of court statement that is not being offered to prove the truth of the statement is not hearsay. (*Evidence Code §1200*; see further discussion of hearsay under the heading Select Legal Authorities).

Example: Fred testifies that Wilma told him she saw defendant kill the victim. Fred's testimony is not admissible because it is being offered to prove that Wilma saw defendant kill the victim.

Personal Knowledge

A witness may not testify to facts unless he personally observed the facts in some way. (*Evidence Code §403.*)

Narrative

Questions should be closed ended and call for short answers on only one subject. A question that calls for a long explanation permits the witness to narrate and is impermissible.

Compound

A question with two subjects is compound and improper. "Did you go to the store and buy a soda?" is compound in that it is asking the witness whether he went to the store and whether he bought a soda.

Speculation

A question that invites the witness to speculate or guess the answer, such as "What was he thinking?" or "What did he do after you left?" The witness cannot know the answer to either of these questions, but can make a logical guess. Such guesses are not allowed, no matter how logical.

Beyond the Scope

A witness first faces direct examination by the party who called the witness to testify. When the other party cross examines the witness, questions are limited to the topic raised by the first party and matters that would tend to impeach the witness.

Calls for a Conclusion

Witnesses must testify to facts, not their opinion as to the facts. It is the duty of the jury or the judge to form conclusions based on the facts as presented. It is, therefore, wrong for a witness to state a conclusion, such as "defendant murdered that man" or "defendant was driving drunk."

Best Evidence

A party trying to prove the contents of a writing can do so by producing the original document or by producing some secondary evidence of the document. However, this secondary evidence cannot be used if "A genuine dispute exists concerning material terms of the writing and justice requires the exclusion" or "Admission of the secondary evidence would be unfair." A Best Evidence objection is claiming that the secondary evidence is inadmissible for one of these two reasons.

In Limine

Objection indicating that a party is violating the court's previous rulings made during hearing of motions in limine.

Vouching

Objection indicating that an attorney is personally vouching for the credibility of a witness.

P. SAMPLE LETTERS

1. Offer to assist

Dear Mr. Canon,

I sent the following information to you to assist in my defense.

I believe it would be beneficial to interview these witnesses:
1. April Anderson – who can testify that the alleged victim previously attacked her.
2. May Smith – who can testify I was with her at the time.
3. June Jones – who can testify that she saw me leave with May.

I believe it would be beneficial to obtain the following evidence:
1. Video recordings from the store where the incident occurred.
2. My phone records to show messages from the alleged victim.

I do not believe that it would be beneficial to check the gun found at the scene for fingerprints or DNA.

Sincerely,

Defendant Don

2. Request for suppression

Dear Mr. Gomez,

Incriminating evidence was taken from my home. After I refused to consent to the search, police entered my home, found evidence, and then detained me while they obtained a warrant. Most of the search was completed prior to the officers obtaining a warrant.

I, therefore, request that you consider bringing a motion to suppress the items taken from my home.

Thank you for your assistance in this matter.

Sincerely,

Dean Dollar

3. Request for discovery

Note:
   Your attorney does not have to give you all of the discovery in your case. There are some items that the attorney cannot physically give you because of custody status, such as CDs, and there are some items the attorney cannot legally give you, such as witness identifying information. For other discovery, it is generally discretionary whether the attorney gives it to you or not. Use this letter as a sample is a request for discovery.

Dear Mr. Jones,

   I would like to participate in my defense. This requires me to have a copy of my discovery. Naturally, I am not requesting confidential witness information or electronic media that cannot be read while I am in custody, but I do need copies of the rest of the discovery in my case.

   Thank you for your assistance in this matter.

> Sincerely,
>
> Defendant Don

4. Request for testing

Dear Mr. Miller,

   I understand that several pieces of evidence were seized in my case, including a gun, a mask, and a pair of gloves.

   I have not touched any of these items. I, therefore, request that you have the items tested for fingerprints and/or DNA as appropriate.

   Thank you for your assistance in this matter.

> Sincerely,
>
> Donny Dank

5. Request to disclose conflicts

Note:
   If you are trying to get rid of your attorney, which is usually a bad idea, this letter and the one that follows may encourage your attorney to declare a conflict of interests. If he is legally obligated to assist someone else concerning your case to the detriment of your case, he must withdraw. This letter is aimed at having your attorney check to see if he has any potential conflicts that could lead to his withdrawal.

Dear Mr. Johnson,

   Thank you for your efforts, but I do not feel that you are giving my case your full attention. I am concerned that you may suffer from a conflict of interests that is preventing you from fully dedicating your efforts to me.

   Please, check your records and let me know whether or not you or anyone from your firm has ever previously represented or currently represents any person in any way that is an alleged victim or witness in my case.

Sincerely,

Douglass Defendant

6. Request to declare conflict

Dear Mr. Ramirez,

   Thank you for your assistance on my case. I trust that you are giving this your best effort, but we simply disagree about my defense, and we are not effectively communicating. I would like to participate in my own defense, but we are not effectively working together.

   I do not wish to bring a Marsden Motion, but I believe it is time that we ended our relationship.

   I hope that we can end the relationship amicably, so I request that you declare a conflict.

Sincerely,

Danny Defendant

7. Request for dismissal

Dear Mr. Mann,

I understand that the prosecution must prove that the value of property was greater than $950. However, at the preliminary hearing, the witness said that the value was, "around $800."

I, therefore, request that you consider bringing a motion to dismiss under Penal Code section 995.

Also, the officer indicated that he recorded my "confession" but accidently erased it. I did not confess. I, therefore, request that you consider bringing a motion to dismiss for lost evidence.

Thank you for your assistance in this matter.

       Sincerely,

       Dean Dollar

∞◊∞◊∞

Every defendant wants his case dismissed. Rumors abound throughout jails and prisons concerning motions to dismiss.

Defendants often ask their attorneys questions like, "Joe's attorney filed a motion to dismiss, and now he's home. Why won't you file a motion to dismiss my case?" Time and again, defendants bring Marsden motions because their attorney won't file a motion to dismiss, but a motion to dismiss is not proper in many cases. Further, there are multiple different types of motion to dismiss, each with its own technical requirements. Some of the more common motions to dismiss are:

- Dismiss in the interest of justice
- Dismiss for speedy trial violation
- Dismiss for delay in prosecution
- Dismiss for loss or destruction of evidence
- Dismiss based on insufficiency of the evidence

The most confusing of these is the Motion to Dismiss in the Interest of Justice, because defendants hear the motion being granted multiple times a day. The motion would be less confusing if it were more properly called a "Motion to Dismiss Because the Defendant Pled to Other Charges."

Q. SELECT LEGAL AUTHORITIES

Evidence Code §350

No evidence is admissible except relevant evidence.

Evidence Code §351

Except as otherwise provided by statute, all relevant evidence is admissible.

Evidence Code §352

The court in its discretion may exclude evidence if its probative value is substantially outweighed by the probability that its admission will
(a) necessitate undue consumption of time or
(b) create substantial danger of undue prejudice, of confusing the issues, or of misleading the jury.

Evidence Code §402

(a) When the existence of a preliminary fact is disputed, its existence or nonexistence shall be determined as provided in this article.
(b) The court may hear and determine the question of the admissibility of evidence out of the presence or hearing of the jury; but in a criminal action, the court shall hear and determine the question of the admissibility of a confession or admission of the defendant out of the presence and hearing of the jury if any party so requests.
(c) A ruling on the admissibility of evidence implies whatever finding of fact is prerequisite thereto; a separate or formal finding is unnecessary unless required by statute.

Evidence Code §1200

(a) "Hearsay evidence" is evidence of a statement that was made other than by a witness while testifying at the hearing and that is offered to prove the truth of the matter stated.
(b) Except as provided by law, hearsay evidence is inadmissible.
(c) This section shall be known and may be cited as the hearsay rule.

There are many exceptions to the hearsay rule that allow hearsay statements to be introduced into evidence. Some of the more common exceptions include:

- *Evidence Code §1220* - Admission of party, such as a defendant's statements
- *Evidence Code §1230* – Declaration against interest, such as a

confession or claim of gang membership.
- *Evidence Code §1235* – Inconsistent statements. A witness's prior statement that contradicts his current testimony can be used against him.
- *Evidence Code §1236* – Prior consistent statements. If a witness's credibility is attacked by showing inconsistencies in his testimony, evidence may be presented to show that the witness previously gave the same version of events.
- *Evidence Code §1237* – Past recollection recorded, such as a report written at the time of an incident that contains details of the incident the witness no longer recalls.
- *Evidence Code §1238* – Prior eye witness identification.
- *Evidence Code §1240* – Spontaneous statement, such as "he shot her!"
- *Evidence Code §1241* – Statement made by declarant explaining his conduct, such as, "I'm going to the store."
- *Evidence Code §1242* – Dying declaration. Statements from a person who believes they are dying regarding the cause of death.
- *Evidence Code §§1250, 1251* – Statement of the speaker's state of mind, such as "I'm tired" or "my leg hurts."
- *Evidence Code §1253* – Statements to medical professionals.
- *Evidence Code §§1271, 1280* – Business records, such as a hotel receipt or a birth certificate.
- *Evidence Code §1291* – Former testimony, such as statements made during a preliminary hearing.
- *Evidence Code §1320, 1324* – The general reputation of a person.
- *Evidence Code §1350* – Statements from a witness made unavailable by the defendant. If a defendant makes a witness unavailable, the witness's prior statements may be used against the defendant.

Penal Code §995

...the indictment or information shall be set aside by the court in which the defendant is arraigned, upon his or her motion [if] the defendant had been committed without reasonable or probable cause.

Penal Code §1054.1

The prosecuting attorney shall disclose to the defendant or his or her attorney all of the following materials and information, if it is in the possession of the prosecuting attorney or if the prosecuting attorney

knows it to be in the possession of the investigating agencies:
(a) The names and addresses of persons the prosecutor intends to call as witnesses at trial.
(b) Statements of all defendants.
(c) All relevant real evidence seized or obtained as a part of the investigation of the offenses charged.
(d) The existence of a felony conviction of any material witness whose credibility is likely to be critical to the outcome of the trial.
(e) Any exculpatory evidence.
(f) Relevant written or recorded statements of witnesses or reports of the statements of witnesses whom the prosecutor intends to call at the trial, including any reports or statements of experts made in conjunction with the case, including the results of physical or mental examinations, scientific tests, experiments, or comparisons which the prosecutor intends to offer in evidence at the trial.

Penal Code §1382

(a) The court, unless good cause to the contrary is shown, shall order the action to be dismissed in the following cases:
  (1) When a person has been held to answer for a public offense and an information is not filed against that person within 15 days.
  (2) In a felony case, when a defendant is not brought to trial within 60 days of the defendant's arraignment on an indictment or information... However, an action shall not be dismissed under this paragraph if either of the following circumstances exists:
      (A) The defendant enters a general waiver of the 60-day trial requirement...
      (B) The defendant requests or consents to the setting of a trial date beyond the 60-day period...
  (3) Regardless of when the complaint is filed, when a defendant in a misdemeanor or infraction case is not brought to trial within 30 days after he or she is arraigned or enters his or her plea, whichever occurs later, if the defendant is in custody at the time of arraignment or plea, whichever occurs later, or in all other cases, within 45 days after the defendant's arraignment or entry of the plea, whichever occurs later... [unless the defendant waives time as noted above]...

Penal Code §1473

(a) A person unlawfully imprisoned or restrained of his or her liberty, under any pretense, may prosecute a writ of habeas corpus to inquire into the cause of his or her imprisonment or restraint.

(b) A writ of habeas corpus may be prosecuted for, but not limited to, the following reasons:

    (1) False evidence that is substantially material or probative on the issue of guilt or punishment was introduced against a person at a hearing or trial relating to his or her incarceration.

    (2) False physical evidence, believed by a person to be factual, probative, or material on the issue of guilt, which was known by the person at the time of entering a plea of guilty, which was a material factor directly related to the plea of guilty by the person.

    (3)

    (A) New evidence exists that is credible, material, presented without substantial delay, and of such decisive force and value that it would have more likely than not changed the outcome at trial.

    (B) For purposes of this section, "new evidence" means evidence that has been discovered after trial, that could not have been discovered prior to trial by the exercise of due diligence, and is admissible and not merely cumulative, corroborative, collateral, or impeaching.

(c) Any allegation that the prosecution knew or should have known of the false nature of the evidence referred to in paragraphs (1) and (2) of subdivision (b) is immaterial to the prosecution of a writ of habeas corpus brought pursuant to paragraph (1) or (2) of subdivision (b).

(d) This section does not limit the grounds for which a writ of habeas corpus may be prosecuted or preclude the use of any other remedies.

(e)

    (1) For purposes of this section, "false evidence" includes opinions of experts that have either been repudiated by the expert who originally provided the opinion at a hearing or trial or that have been undermined by later scientific research or technological advances.

    (2) This section does not create additional liabilities, beyond those already recognized, for an expert who repudiates his or her original opinion provided at a hearing or trial or whose opinion has been undermined by later scientific research or technological advancements.

A habeas corpus petition can be used to challenge the validity of a conviction or the conditions of confinement at the jail.

Penal Code §1473 is included in this book because it has been requested so many times, but a habeas corpus petition is almost always the wrong thing to file prior to a defendant being convicted and appealing the conviction.

Penal Code §1538.5

(a) (1) A defendant may move for the return of property or to suppress as evidence any tangible or intangible thing obtained as a result of a search or seizure on either of the following grounds:
    (A) The search or seizure without a warrant was unreasonable.
    (B) The search or seizure with a warrant was unreasonable because any of the following apply:
        (i) The warrant is insufficient on its face.
        (ii) The property or evidence obtained is not that described in the warrant.
        (iii) There was not probable cause for the issuance of the warrant.
        (iv) The method of execution of the warrant violated federal or state constitutional standards.
        (v) There was any other violation of federal or state constitutional standards…

∞◊∞◊∞

Penal Code §1538.5 codifies and explains the Fourth Amendment prohibition against unreasonable searches and seizures by government officials. It does not apply to searches conducted by private citizens, such as security guards. If a store security guard conducts a search, it does not implicate the Fourth Amendment and suppression is not available under *Penal Code §1538.5*.

R. ABOUT THE AUTHORS

Roger Lampkin

Roger Lampkin earned his bachelor degree from University of Texas at Austin. His Juris Doctor degree is from South Texas College of Law where he was editor of the Law Review, and where he was an adjunct professor after graduation. Mr. Lampkin became an attorney in Texas in 1973 and in California in 1984. He has published various award winning articles. After coming to California, he was an adjunct professor in a California law school and taught a legally orientated course at California State University.

From 1973 to 1987, Mr. Lampkin was in the legal department of major oil companies supervising outside counsel in substantial litigation. He entered private practice in 1987 and has offices in Bakersfield and Taft. He is licensed to practice in Texas, California, and Federal Courts. His successful representation of thousands of clients has included extensive trial experience; where he learned the importance of pretrial motions and became highly skilled at preparing and arguing all necessary and essential motions. A trial may be won or lost at the motions stage, when the "ground rules" for the conduct of trial are set.

J. Anthony Bryan

Mr. Bryan is an attorney who received his bachelor degree from San Francisco State University and his Juris Doctor degree from Loyola Law School.

He is an author of *Sex Registration Guidebook*, and he has been successfully representing criminal defendants for over forty years. Mr. Bryan has also been a city prosecutor, so he knows how things work on both sides of a case.

Mr. Bryan received his Honorable Discharge from the United States Marine Corps in 1965, and is also a former firefighter with the United States Forest Service. Mr. Bryan was once described by the Bakersfield Californian as the "Courtroom Tornado," and he was the winner of the 2003 Atticus Finch Award for "unwavering commitment to his clients and the law." He is highly skilled in criminal defense, and has been appointed by the court on dozens of death penalty cases. When a defendant's life is on the line, courts and clients trust Mr. Bryan.

Made in United States
Orlando, FL
19 March 2022